FIND
YOUR
INNER
UGLY BETTY

FIND YOUR INNER UGLY BETTY

25 Career Lessons for Young
Professionals Inspired by TV Shows

TANNER STRANSKY

KAPLAN PUBLISHING

New York

Vice President and Publisher: Maureen McMahon
Editorial Director: Jennifer Farthing
Acquisitions Director: Susan Barry
Acquisitions Editor: Shannon Berning
Production Editor: Dominique Polfliet
Production Designer: Ivelisse Robles Marrero
Cover Designer: Carly Schnur

© 2008 Tanner Stransky

Published by Kaplan Publishing, a division of Kaplan, Inc.
1 Liberty Plaza, 24th Floor
New York, NY 10006

Printed in the United States of America

May 2008
10 9 8 7 6 5 4 3 2 1

ISBN-13: 978-1-4277-9767-4

Kaplan Publishing books are available at special quantity discounts to use for sales promotions, employee premiums, or educational purposes. Please email our Special Sales Department to order or for more information at kaplanpublishing@kaplan.com, or write to Kaplan Publishing, 1 Liberty Plaza, 24th Floor, New York, NY 10006.

Contents

Part Three: Become Irreplaceable

Part Four: Go Beyond Office Hours

Part Five: Advance Your Career

Introduction

As an entertainment journalist on the television beat, I regularly pass off my obsessive TV-watching as an interest that's good for my career. But while doing my "research," I couldn't help but notice that young professionals dominate primetime.

Just think: There's *Ugly Betty*, the crew on *30 Rock*, the Dunder Mifflin dolts on *The Office*, the hip cluster of friends on *How I Met Your Mother*, the amorous doctors on *Grey's Anatomy*, and a riddled young lawyer on *Damages* just to name a handful of the most popular shows. To get historical for a moment, decades of young careerists—from Mary Richards on *The Mary Tyler Moore Show* to the more recently departed crew on *Friends*—have depicted and influenced the way generations clock in and out. America loves seeing young, rising professionals on the small screen.

Admittedly, these dramas and comedies are crafted to entertain, as antics often spiral into the outlandish. But at the same time, I came to realize the messages they provide also inadvertently include career advice on everything from proper office etiquette to having networking prowess and a whole host of other topics.

Take *Grey's Anatomy*, a drama about interns-cum-doctors in Seattle, for instance: Meredith Grey's romance with McDreamy reminds us of the pitfalls of dating a coworker, while Christina Yang's over-the-top eagerness shows the advantages of going the extra mile. Ellen Parsons, an enterprising young attorney on *Damages*, teaches us about the importance of mentorship and making a graceful exit when leaving a job. *30 Rock*'s Liz Lemon proves you can have a good, mentoring relationship with your boss—even if it is unconventional. Then there are examples less focused on the actual workplace: Just like *Friends* before it, *How I Met Your Mother* depicts a tight-knit group of young professionals who support each other off the job. Naturally, what not to do is raucously on display too: The antics on *The Office*—and mostly boss Michael Scott's awkward doings—are a full-out education in the workplace gone awry.

Of all the shows out there, however, *Ugly Betty* provides us with one of the strongest models of how to get ahead. Betty Suarez is the icon for our generation, just as Mary Tyler Moore was for a previous one. Betty is an awkward young professional whose star is rising.

From the day she waltzed into the offices of *Mode*, the odds were stacked against her. She was the local Queens girl transplanted to the cutthroat world of Manhattan corporate culture who naively reported to her first day at work wearing a

Guadalajara poncho, a toothy grin framed with shiny braces, and strawberry-tinged horn-rimmed glasses—a risky move at a glitzy fashion magazine akin to *Vogue*.

But despite some faux pas, Betty is a model employee you can learn from: She's spot-on with every assignment, she has a great relationship with her boss, and she's moving and shaking every day toward a promotion. It may just take a little digging to bring your inner Ugly Betty to life, but that's why I'm here to help.

See, I'm a Betty too. Much like her, I'm new to the working world and figuring out this whole corporate thing. Right after graduating from Drake University in 2005, I moved to New York City to pursue my dream of becoming an entertainment magazine reporter or editor. My eyes were set toward working at *Entertainment Weekly*, but I quickly learned that even the lowest positions at the prestigious magazine usually went to folks with a couple years of post-collegiate experience. So, employing that same can-do spirit that drives the likes of Betty and the legions of young professionals on television, I started plugging away: I spent over a year working at a small television magazine before snagging a gig at the *New York Post*. The beat wasn't entertainment, but it served to bulk up my resume, until the powers that be at *EW* finally noticed.

Now, I write and report about television, with the occasional book review, movie preview, or style dissection thrown in for good measure.

Beyond working at *EW*, I further my career by volunteering for a networking group called Ed2010 (www.ed2010.com), which caters to young editors striving to reach their dream magazine job. The group is built around networking events and educational panels. I run the part of the organization that caters to students in journalism schools who hope to become editors in New York City one day.

All of this career knowledge, work experience, and television watching prepared me to write this book. Anchored in critiques of pop culture's young professionals—from Pam Beesly to Betty Suarez—I've created a manual of how to get ahead in the workplace. I examined their on-screen actions and asked myself, "What can a work-bound college graduate take away from what these television personalities are doing?" Then, to anchor it in the real world, I asked dozens of real-life "Bettys" and a batch of the nation's top career experts for their insight too.

Whether you work in law, finance, nursing, media, or another field, there's something here for you. *Find Your Inner Ugly Betty* contains 25 lessons to help you polish your image, build solid business relationships, become irreplaceable, go beyond office hours, and advance your career.

Read on to find your inner Ugly Betty—it's in there, even if it needs a little help to bust out! As for me, I'm gonna flip on my DVR and get back to my obsessive TV-watching. You should, too, because—coupled with this book—it may just turn out to be a darn good career move.

Part One

Polish Your Image

LESSON 1
Kill 'Em with Confidence

"You are an attractive, intelligent, confident businesswoman."

—*Betty Suarez, prepping herself before her first staff meeting at* Mode, *on* Ugly Betty

Think back to when *Ugly Betty's* Betty Suarez was given her first real writing assignment for *Mode*. Sitting in a swank hotel room with the task of reviewing the accommodations for the magazine, Betty was visibly nervous and questioned whether she had a clue about how to tackle the task. She hemmed and hawed and went around in circles, doubting herself. In the end, however, she handled the situation with textbook precision and turned in a review that eventually ran in one of *Mode's* sister magazines at Meade Publications. What Betty did—gain confidence and become unafraid to wield it—is what you'll have to do time and time again.

In your first few months on the job—and probably throughout other stages of your career—your confidence level is going to be at the big, fat goose egg of zero. An assignment will come down the pipeline to you, and you'll sit there staring at it, thinking, where the hell do I even start? But this is where your unshakable confidence comes in: It's imperative that you stay strong and believe in what you do. You definitely know your stuff, but everyone has moments of being flustered. So here's your plan instead of fretting: Take a deep breath, think things through, put on your game face, and get to it.

Put on Your Poker Face

Or, as they say, fake it until you can make it. If there's one essential takeaway from this chapter, it's simply to *look* confident. Even if you're quaking inside, mask it. Smile until your face hurts, nod your head in agreement, and, for goodness sakes, don't let your voice crack.

I had to pull out my poker face frequently during my first few months at *Entertainment Weekly*, a magazine environment with similarities to Betty's *Mode*. Here's just one example: On my third day at *EW*, I was assigned the task of soliciting the cast and crew of Lindsay Lohan's newest movie, *Georgia Rule*, to see if I could get any scoop about her alleged absenteeism on set. And no joke, the folks I was targeting had voice mails that included "do not solicit" threats to reporters, so this was no easy task. Though I'd had several internships and post-collegiate jobs, I'd never stalked people like this before, and I had no idea what I was doing. However, when my editor came to me with the task, I smiled, nodded my head, and then fretted only *after* she trotted away. I wanted her to know that I could handle the responsibility.

Looking confident is all about nonverbal cues, like smiling, says Dan King, a career counselor and principal of Boston's Career Planning and Management, Inc., who warns that so many little things—such as grimacing, groaning, even flickering your eyes when you're uncomfortable—can cast the wrong image.

"A lot of projecting of confidence is not even the verbal stuff," King says. "It's all in the facial expressions, the posture, the body language, and the mannerisms." He suggests zeroing in on one such problem area at a time: "Holding your head up rather than looking down at the floor can make all the difference in the world."

Then, repeat, correcting your posture, nervous tics, facial expressions, and so on. Bottom line: Pay attention to what your actions are in relation to your confidence level. If the vibe you're giving off isn't one of total assurance, consider altering what you're doing.

Be Fearless! Not Arrogant or Smug

A can-do attitude should come naturally as you settle into your new position and become more comfortable and competent. But beware: If you're not careful, that much-needed know-how can morph into confidence's ugly twin, arrogance. And, believe me, *no one* likes the office prima donna. Just look at braggart supreme Michael Scott from *The Office* for a prime example of ego overriding confidence. His employees can't stand him, and it's the same for employees who project such an air.

Just realizing the distinction between confidence and arrogance usually will keep you from dark waters. "People who come across as truly overbearing and arrogant never give it a second thought," says King. Michael Scott has no idea of his rampant self-importance and, thus, won't ever be able to fix it. "The fact that you're giving it a second thought and saying, 'I don't want to appear overbearing,' means you never will."

You Know Your Stuff, So Just Do It

As much as you may want to doubt yourself, especially when you start your job, remember that your bosses brought you into the fold because you have what it takes. Now, put those skills and your good sense to the task.

Tiffany, a 23-year-old nurse on a stressful oncology floor in a Las Vegas hospital, battled self-doubt at first, even though her years of training meant she definitely had acquired the skill set. Three days into her new position, she had one of many first tests. Without getting too specific and gruesome, she had to stick a long needle into a patient's chemotherapy port carefully enough so he wouldn't feel it. She'd practiced the procedure on dummies dozens of times before. But when it came time for the real deal—her test, if you will—Tiffany "felt like crying I was so scared." Just before she started the procedure, her boss pulled her aside and told her that, even though she was nervous, she had to do it—otherwise, she'd never learn. And, voila, success!

The conundrum is akin to the one *How I Met Your Mother*'s young lawyer Marshall faced when he swore he couldn't pass the bar exam. The doubt was bringing him down, in the same way it did with Tiffany, while, in fact, he did pass. "Once I did it, I felt like I could do anything," Tiffany says. "I didn't have this cloud hanging over me anymore. Even though I was so new, just tackling it head-on helped me more than anything."

As a final piece of advice on building confidence, King has this to add: "You need to make sure that you're at least giving yourself credit for what you do. If you don't believe you bring some value to your organization or to a job, you're going to have a hard time getting anyone else to see it."

The fact is that you *do* have the ability to meet and exceed your own expectations, but taking that first terrifying step toward success is the hardest part. Put on your poker face, lose the arrogance, and just do it. Trust me, you'll succeed.

And, if you're overly confident, don't miss lesson 3: Watch Your Mouth.

On the Job
• • • • •

Scenario: Two months into your new job in the finance industry, you're assigned to make a presentation to a few of your department's managing directors. You're understandably freaking out, but what's the best way to approach the situation?

✳

Quick Fix: Grab the bull by the horns! Take the assignment and don't let your boss think for a minute that it's something you can't handle. Study up and master those nonverbal cues that show your confidence, then make the presentation. You'll be proud of yourself after you've brazenly tackled it with great success.

Real-Life "Betty"

"With teaching, you have to fake confidence at first. And even if you do have it, you're going to get humbled! I remember how sick I felt on the first day right before the kids came in. It was pretty much just sheer terror. But I *smiled* through it and made sure I was prepared every day and stayed as consistent as I could. Eventually, the image I had of myself turned into real confidence. That doesn't mean I never got humbled again— something new happens even on the most routine day! Parent-teacher conferences are the same way, but I don't think that ever changes for most teachers. Projecting confidence projects competence. People want to see that their child's teacher is effective, and of course, it's important that you are."

—*Kylie, 24, Texas*

• • • • • •

To-Do List

* **Smile and make direct eye contact**. You instantly appear ten times more competent.

* **Have an opening line handy**. You'll be much more likely to strike up a conversation or say hello if you've got a few introductory lines in your arsenal.

* **Shake hands early and often**. Always stand up and be the first to offer your hand for the obligatory handshake.

* **Fake it**. Forge the confidence and focus on your skills and abilities. The self-doubt will fall away naturally.

* **Monitor your nonverbal cues**. Sighing, hanging your head, or a puny handshake show weakness and lack of enthusiasm.

* **Become fearless through actions**. Just like with Tiffany, the nurse from Las Vegas, confidence and competence come after you've taken a stab at the task and risen to the challenge.

* **Avoid arrogance**. Always be assured, but humble.

* **Follow the leader**. Nervous about what to do? Get into line and mimic the actions of those around you.

* **Be prepared**. You'll never have an excuse to wuss out of a situation.

* **Take risks when possible**. The bigger the risk, the greater the potential for return.

* **Remember: Everyone is a human being**. We all have fears and insecurities.

Embrace Your Individual Style

"I admit it's tempting to wish for the perfect boss or the perfect parent or the perfect outfit, but maybe the best any of us can do is not quit, play the hand we've been given, and accessorize the outfit we've got."

—*Carrie Bradshaw, theorizing during her freelance gig at* Vogue, *on* Sex and the City

A sage mentor of mine once told me that you have five seconds to make a good impression. So, armed with that advice and the above wisdom from *Sex and the City*'s savvy style queen Carrie Bradshaw, you better look darn good when you're at work. For better or worse, how you dress determines how coworkers and your boss perceive you. And why shouldn't it? Your wardrobe, and the space you work in—whether it's a cube, office, classroom, or otherwise—are the two things that *immediately* contribute to that all-important first impression.

In terms of her personal style, super-successful professional Carrie resigned herself to play the hand she was dealt. In other words, she's decided to *own* her style—and you should too. Betty certainly does: Just look at that loud Guadalajara poncho she wore on her first day at *Mode*. True, it can be career suicide to strut into your office wearing outfits like Betty's—her wicked coworker Marc curtly slugged her ill-advised choice a "killer poncho"—but there is an important lesson in both of these characters' fashion forwardness: They're not confused with any of their colleagues. Instead, they're unique and stand out. Take your work situation into account, though: You may not want to stand out quite as much as these two fashionistas. Being noticed isn't a good thing if it isn't for a positive reason. But your personal style, in some form, has a place in the office, even if the environment is restrained. You want to tell your coworkers who you are—in the words of Carrie, "accessorize the outfit you've got" but still make sure the message is clear: "I'm competent."

Expressing yourself through fashion directly affects your confidence level. When you're comfortable, you look good. When you look good, you feel good about yourself and, ultimately, perform better. The first step toward feeling comfortable concerns understanding the do's and don'ts in your office. Only then can you decide how to fittingly Bettify, or add a little Bradshaw, to your wardrobe.

Assess Your Workplace's Vibe

Unless you're relegated to standard-issue style, like the scrubs-clad doctors of *Grey's Anatomy*, you've got some wardrobe decisions to make. Start with assessing your workplace, which is the only way you'll know if you're making a Betty-sized blunder.

It is probably best to go a tad conservative at first, especially if you're concerned with making too big a splash. Envision your office's style on a sliding scale of 1 to 5, with 5 being most conservative. It's best if you stay to the top of the scale during your initial weeks.

As Jessica, a 23-year-old publicist in New York City, says, "You can *never* be too professionally dressed. I've never heard a boss say, 'Can you believe he or she wore a suit?' But I've heard them many, many times comment on someone who was underdressed." As you figure out the norm, taper off of the stiff-necked suits into clothes that'll work best for you—and show your personality.

Once you've evaluated your company's official policy on dress, here's a list of wardrobe-related questions to ask yourself:

- What do my colleagues at my level wear on a typical day?
- What does my boss wear on a regular basis?
- Do my coworkers dress up on certain days, such as for meetings, presentations, or when clients are in the office?
- Are Fridays casual? If so, exactly *how* casual?
- Is a statement of individual style valued in this environment? If so, how are my colleagues personalizing their wardrobe? How can I fit in yet still feel individual?

- Is it worth rocking the boat in terms of fashion? Could my fashion choices possibly draw unnecessary attention?
- How can I make a statement of individual style while still casting a professional image that also projects competence?

Answer these questions, and you'll be on the track to knowing what's in and what's out at your office.

Infuse Your Own Flavor Where Possible

After you determine what flies around your office, the next—and hugely important!—step is to decide how to infuse your flavor into your wardrobe. Bernadette Fitzpatrick, vice president and creative director for makeup giant Sephora in New York City, says the best way to do that is to take a cue from the working girls of *Sex and the City*. "Accessorize, accessorize, accessorize!" is her mantra.

Fitzpatrick adds, "From my own experience, I think it's really important—especially in the business world, where everyone dresses so generically—to add some personal flavor." Whether you work in Fashionista Central or Frumpy Crossing, there are five easily adjustable parts of your look you can quickly tweak to show your personal flair:

Under that jacket. If suits are standard, wear a shirt or blouse in a popping color or eye-catching pattern or print. This will rarely offend but can do wonders for your overall look.

Bags. Because you don't typically drag your purse or messenger bag into meetings—rather, they probably just sit under your desk most of the day—feel free to have fun with them. Again, it's appropriate to infuse a little of your personal style here. Pick hues that pop against the more neutral tones of your base garments.

Shoes. Of course, shoot for a mix of comfort and practicality. But why not try footwear with a special touch, like a shiny buckle, bow, or dazzling color? "Shoes are the best way to make you stand out," Fitzpatrick adds.

Hair. Depending on how liberal the standards are around your office, guys can go shaggy or even add some color. Girls, show your fashion sense with a funky flowered or beaded headband.

Accessories. Guys, have a bit of fun with your cuff links, suspenders, and belt. They're tiny parts of your overall look, but they can easily jazz up an ensemble. If outwardly stylish accoutrements won't fly in your office, wear socks that make you smile. No one else is going to see them anyway. Gals, you can play with patterned scarves, bracelets, and jewelry. In terms of jewelry, however, avoid anything that will jangle and, thus, make too much noise. You want your style to stand out, just not for the sounds it may be making!

Dress Up Your Space Too

As a final note on style, infusing your personality at work goes beyond just the clothes on your back. Think about your office too: What does that drunken frat-party photo on your bulletin board say to colleagues who stop by your desk? Is that glittery pen with a poofball on the end instead of an eraser really the message you want to send? What about all those empty cans of Red Bull—do they mean you regularly have to jolt yourself into completing work? Your wardrobe is grown-up, so your workspace should be too.

Ideally, your desk and office should be neat and clean yet still reflect who you are. Because you'll be there at least 40 hours a week—and likely more—it's a space to make personal because it's, in essence, an extension of yourself. Photos of family or friends, knick-knacks that mean something to you, and your favorite magazines are appropriate, but veer away from becoming that office dweller with wacky trinkets.

On the Job
• • • • •

Problem: You're new to your nonprofit office and still getting a grip on the dress code. There's no written protocol, and your officemates show up wearing all sorts of garb—from low-cut halter tops to frumpy dresses that should have been left in the decade in which they were originally designed. Everyone is all over the place! Who should you take your style cues from?

✳

Quick Fix: Yourself! In this interesting situation, you really have the opportunity to channel your own style, more so than in more restrained work environments. So you should go for it! The style slate is blank here, so it's safe for you to experiment to your heart's content.

Real-Life "Betty"

"My first week of work at the law firm, I didn't exactly have a lot to wear. It was my first job, and I had mostly leftover college duds. I thought, Maybe it's time I invest in some business-wear to dress the part. So I bought some great outfits—collared shirts and black skirts. Not giving it a second thought, I wore my best one the next day. I was just so happy it fit and looked good! The first thing I hear is, 'Oh, Jillian, we forgot to tell you that it's casual Friday!' Every person who saw me in my awesome outfit that day was *nice* enough to remind me that Fridays are always casual. It's a simple, silly lesson, but you should always ask around about Fridays. More often than not, they're casual."

—*Jillian, 25, Houston*

• • • • • •

To-Do List

* **Make a good first impression**. You've only got one shot, so make it count.

* **Start conservative**. Reign in your style at first, then get more adventurous as you figure out the vibe of the office.

* **Figure out your office's de facto dress code**. Don't just follow the employee manual. Check out what your bosses and coworkers are wearing and follow suit—literally, if that's the case.

* **Show personality selectively**. Smaller items—shirts beneath your suit jacket, bags, shoes, hair, and accessories—are the easiest areas to inject your personal flair.

* **Ask colleagues what goes**. You might be surprised to hear what they have to say. Check in about the possibility of casual Fridays too.

* **Pay attention to the details**. Dirty fingernails, scuffed shoes, and wrinkly shirts are never in at work.

* **Clean up after a night out**. Young office manager Lena on *Brothers & Sisters* has done it many a time, but it's never okay to show up at work smelling of liquor and cigarettes after a night of hard partying. Alternatively, Fitzpatrick advises, "Remember that the office is not a nightclub. How you dress to go out *after* work is not necessarily the best outfit *for* work."

* **Go cheap**. Not in looks, but in price! It's your first job, so there's no shame in shopping at budget-conscious but trendy stores, such as H&M or Forever 21, to add a splash of affordable, personal flavor to your wardrobe.

* **Keep makeup low-key**. Save your bright-red lips and raccoon eyes for the clubs.

* **Dress for the job you want**. You'll be more quickly promoted if your boss can visualize you in your dream job.

* **Make your personal space your own**. Just remember to keep it professional.

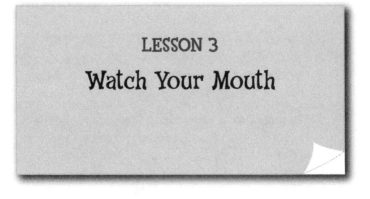

LESSON 3

Watch Your Mouth

"Hold on a second. I think Pam wanted to say something. Pam? You had a look like you wanted to ask a question just then."

—*Michael Scott, wondering whether his receptionist Pam Beesly wanted to pipe up, on* The Office

To speak up or stay quiet, that is the question. In new work environs, knowing when it's appropriate for you to pipe up is daunting. Speaking out of turn can be a major faux pas that could haunt you for a long time. At the same time, missing an opportunity to add your two cents can be just as bad and make you seem like a noncontributor. So what's a peppy young professional brimming with ideas to do? Use restraint and follow your instincts. Generally speaking, if it feels natural for you to spring to life in a meeting or at a gathering, go for it, especially if that seems like standard procedure among your colleagues. If you've got any sense, you'll most likely know when the time isn't so appropriate.

Take Pam, the soft-spoken receptionist from *The Office*, as an example of an employee who knows how to manage her mouth. She speaks up when something needs to be said and restrains herself during situations where butting in might just entice her loud-mouthed boss Michael to continue being inappropriate. Her job doesn't require her to get involved in office meetings to the extent of the other employees, but she still contributes in a smart, put together way, just like you should.

Know When to Speak Up and When to Shut Up

Just as you assessed the fashion situation at work, you've got to do the same with the mouthing-off protocol around the office. What's the norm? Are employees encouraged to speak up at all times? Is there a particular time and place?

For the most part, you can use your instincts: Certain situations beg for you to jump into the conversations. Those *usually* include circumstances such as brainstorming sessions; one-on-one, closed-door meetings; and situations where what you say will directly affect your company's bottom line. But not always: Keeping quiet might be appropriate in those cases too. It's important to *at the least* understand that you're walking a very slippery slope. Of course, many murky areas exist, but, as executive coach Maria Marsala of Poulsbo, Washington, says, "A good rule of thumb is that if it doesn't feel right to you, keep your mouth shut."

But then again, you can speak up forcefully in a tasteful way too. In her first few weeks of work, Kylie, the second-grade teacher from Texas who we met in lesson 1, was presented with a conundrum: Her team of teachers was putting on what she felt was an inaccurate play about Thanksgiving, which featured a Pilgrim-Native Americans dinner after which everyone lived happily ever after. "I felt like we were presenting the students a lie," she says.

So what'd she do? Rather than mouth off about it at a rehearsal and cause a scene, she aired her concerns in a closed-door meeting at a later time. "I explained to my colleagues that I felt we were doing our diverse students a disservice by presenting that story as history." But, as you might expect, saying her piece wasn't simply that easy: "It was tough not to get upset and emotional, especially since it was really the first time I had had any sort of say in any job, but I think they were willing to listen because I kept my head up. We did choose a new play, and it was a huge success."

In this situation, Kylie had to weigh how important her convictions were to her against a possible negative reaction by the other teachers. It could have gone woefully wrong, if she hadn't been so conscientious about when and where to air her concerns. In the end, speaking her mind—much like the spirited young Mary Richards often did on *The Mary Tyler Moore Show*—paid off huge dividends for Kylie, who was praised for how she handled the situation: "A colleague I respected very much told me afterwards that she really admired my courage, and she didn't think she could have done the same thing in her first year."

When you do speak up, "Say what you mean and mean what you say," advises Jennifer Johnson, founder of image consulting service All About You Enterprises in Overland Park, Kansas, and member of the public speaking group Toastmasters International. "That is so important because I think, needless to say, everything else follows that from the standpoint of building your credibility with people. It's about your integrity and your character. If you're going to do something and you tell people you're going to do something, make sure it's true. It's just being up front, being honest."

Make Your Words Positive!

If you don't have something nice to say, don't say anything at all. Remember when your kindergarten teacher told you that on the first day of elementary school? Well, in a workplace setting, the heart of the advice still applies, especially when you're making comments that aren't behind closed doors.

Being negative and forgetting her filter burned 25-year-old Cate at the small New York City literary agency where she is an assistant. She took her negative complaint to an all-staff meeting, where it backfired.

"I, always the foolhardy one, decided that this was the time to bring up my own quandary," Cate says. "I told everyone that they were getting far too many personal phone calls during the day. So, here I am the newest assistant on the block, chiding all my bosses and coworkers for getting too many personal calls."

It was totally the wrong setting to bring up a complaint, but luckily for Cate, it didn't affect her job *that* much. "Everyone held in laughter to salvage my feelings, but to this day—almost two years later—my coworkers will loudly exclaim as I walk by, 'Just one moment, I'm on a personal call!' or 'Oh, I'm sorry, this is personal!'"

However, Cate learned a valuable lesson: "I learned that in office-wide meetings, even in small offices like mine, you should run your complaints by someone before you make them."

On the Job
• • • • •

Scenario: You're a young accountant in a large firm in Los Angeles and have a brilliant idea about improving a system in your office that'll make operations move much, much smoother and increase productivity. What's the best way to let someone know about your concept?

✳

Quick Fix: While your first instinct may be to pitch it at a staff meeting, resist—especially because you'd probably be speaking out of turn and could possibly offend the person who created the current system. In this situation, just like when Betty pitched her winning Fabia Cosmetics spread idea, write up a proposal and go directly to your boss. This is a situation for a one-on-one pitch initially. Your boss can help you bring your idea to fruition smoothly. Plus, if it's a total flop, you haven't embarrassed yourself in front of your entire office.

Real-Life "Betty"

"The honeymoon phase at my new consulting job was over. It was time to really begin proving myself—and my salary. My boss called me and said he was putting me on a new, high-profile client team with two fast-rising managing directors overseeing my work. I was excited. But I was a bit too excited. In our first meeting with the client, I came off like I was the third managing director and spoke up too much. I didn't realize it, but I was simply expected to be quiet and let the 'star' team members carry the verbal load. Two weeks later, I was pulled from the project. So much for proving myself. No one told me explicitly, but later on I heard through another managing director that it was seen as my not knowing how to 'play my role.' Ever since, I've realized the importance of working by this rule: When you're the lowest ranking person in the room, only speak if you have something to say that's going to make some money for the client, save the client from spending money, or save your team from looking dumb—not just because you want to show how smart you are."

—*Joah, 25, Washington, D.C.*

• • • • • •

To-Do List

* **Know your role**. If you're supposed to be a fly on the wall, it's probably best not to buzz into business where you have no place.

* **Go with your gut**. Your instincts usually will be right about whether it's an appropriate time for you to add your two cents.

* **Avoid finishing the sentence of someone who's talking**. It's tacky, rude, and usually will blow up in your face.

* **If you don't have anything nice to say, don't say anything at all**. You can't go wrong with positive public speaking.

* **Air touchy concerns or complaints behind closed doors**. It's unprofessional to call coworkers or—gasp!—your boss to task in front of others.

Guard Your Personal Brand

"I don't want to be, like, a guy here, you know? Like Stanley is 'The Crossword Puzzle Guy,' and Angela has cats. I don't want to have a thing here."

—*Dunder Mifflin employee Ryan Howard, on* The Office

It's weird to think of yourself as a "brand," right? But what I'm talking about here is your reputation. What springs to mind when your boss and coworkers think of you? In the quote above, Dunder Mifflin's Ryan hopes to avoid being pegged with a cliché title like so many of his officemates. But, as any career expert or working professional would tell him, that's nearly impossible to escape. People love labels and naturally gravitate toward slotting their coworkers with one, whether it's "The Tech-Savvy Guy" or "The Weekend Partier." Or, as in Ryan's case, after he started a fire in the office kitchen, "The Fire Guy." Betty Suarez of *Ugly Betty* was quickly tagged a "Fashion Victim."

So who are you going to be? Especially in the early days of your job, you have the power to shape perceptions. Mull over the ammunition you're giving your coworkers and do what you can to make sure it's positive. Would you rather be "The Peace Keeper" or "The Workhorse"? "The Team Player" or "The Lazy One"? It's all about molding your image and reputation the right way, which, with a little help, you easily can do.

The Small Stuff Defines You

Simple actions, such as the distinctive habits you develop, affect how you're perceived. Career counselor Dan King says you should expect everything you do during business hours to be assessed by a coworker or a boss.

"What do you look like when you eat your lunch? Do you chew loudly with your mouth open?" he questions. "It's all very important. If you're seeing lunch with somebody as a chance to chow down—wrong. If you're going out to lunch with someone, maybe you need to eat a little bit before you go to lunch so you don't go there and eat like a raving lunatic."

It seems asinine that such rudimentary things would come to define you, but as the staff designations on *The Office* unfortunately point out in a lavishly exaggerated fashion, it's usually the most unsavory acts that define you. Deborah Ohrn, an editor-in-chief at magazine publisher Meredith Corporation, Des Moines, Iowa, encourages young professionals to voraciously protect their brand.

"Image is the whole package; it's the brand. You've got to protect yours," she says. "It's sad to say, but senior management goes into that whole image, including the looks and the persona to how you do a presentation. I've got a variety of brilliant young people, and some don't have a clue how to package themselves in the office. They're late and disheveled. They stroll in an hour after they're expected and they're like, 'Oh sorry.' I'm like, 'We were waiting for you at nine and it's 10:12.' It just adds up to a poor view of them overall, despite their skills."

Most importantly, "You need to understand how you're perceived," adds King. "Most people think, 'Well doesn't everybody see me the way I do?' No, they really don't. If you haven't had an opportunity to take a look at yourself closely, do it. You might just be surprised and want to change a few things."

Clean Up Your Online Image

You likely built your MySpace or Facebook homepages when you were in college and, naturally, didn't flinch when your friends tagged you in photos where you're clearly three sheets to the wind or upside down on a keg stand. Even Betty dubiously put herself out there for scrutiny by colleagues by posting a profile on a dating website. Just like you, Betty should have realized that in today's tech-savvy professional world, bosses and coworkers would undoubtedly see the information, regardless of whether it was actually intended for them.

I honestly can say I was startled when I logged in to Facebook a few months into my gig at *Entertainment Weekly* and found all my superiors had their own pages too. For a time, I had convinced myself that my bosses or other contacts in my industry were too old and would never be able to find me in such forums. I quickly cleaned up all the photos, comments, and information I had put out there, removing anything that was remotely unsavory. My bosses don't need to know what I do over the weekend, especially if it portrays me in a bad light.

If you're adamant about leaving those hard-partying photos up, you may be able to change the privacy settings on your site. It's smart to limit access for work acquaintances. Although, yes, you're an adult and obviously cuss, drink, and—gasp!—even have sex just like your bosses, laying out all the gory details of your personal life for them is, without question, vulgar.

Develop a "Classic You" Calling Card

Because you basically have a clean slate when you walk into your new job, strike while the iron is hot. The first few weeks is the prime time to develop what I'm calling a "classic you" calling card, or a distinguishing characteristic or behavior that you're known for amongst your coworkers and superiors. Be sure to make the association positive.

It could be as simple as you billing yourself as the go-to person for Excel expertise or that coworker who always brings in homemade chocolate chip pistachio cookies on Friday mornings. Or how about fashioning yourself into the gal who can churn out a stellar idea in five seconds?

"It's a misconception to believe it's a bad thing to be known for something around the office," says Ohrn. "I love my go-to people, and I utilize them all the time. You have control of how you're perceived—especially in that three- to six-month window right after you're hired—so coming up with something you're known for that your boss and co-workers associate in a positive light is key."

Tory, who scored her first job as an art director at the age of 22 in Chicago, had the latitude to unabashedly be herself and it worked to her advantage. "I baked banana bread and cupcakes for the office," she remembers. "I went rollerblading and swimming in Lake Michigan on my lunch breaks, and brought back seashells for my coworkers. They loved it! I dressed the same way I've always dressed: a style loosely based off the philosophy of 'If I'm not having fun wearing it, then I don't want to wear it.' And, surprisingly enough, my fashion sense became a sort of requested form of office entertainment and a calling card: I was often asked to wear the stripey leggings for a certain event or was introduced to various clients on a 'you've gotta check this out' basis. My 'free hugs' t-shirt was a popular favorite, especially around the end of winter when people got droopy."

On the Job
• • • • •

Scenario: You've been on the job for three months and, granted you're still new, you're having a hard time feeling like you're making an impact. No one seems to know who you are or what you're about, despite your best efforts. What can you do to build your personal brand?

✳

Quick Fix: Decide what your strength is and play to it: What are you best at? Where do you have contacts that you can work? What aspect of your job do you get the most compliments for? Figure all that out and then work it!

Real-Life "Betty"

"I had just landed a plum job as an art director, replacing an employee who had been there for 20 years. I knew that to meet the expectations of the job, a great deal about my mannerisms and tendencies would have to change to fit this new role. I had to learn how to speak to clients with sensitivity and professionalism; how to give a presentation with poise; how to sell my ideas with confidence and showmanship; and how to take a stand and defend it. I learned how to meet the expectations without changing who I was. They hired a whole person, you know? I thought they deserved the whole package—like, *everything* you can bring to the table, not just your skills. There's *so* very much that goes into building a workplace besides just skills. And those elements will be what keep people happy and healthy and excited to be there and willing to stay."

—*Tory, 25, Chicago*

• • • • • •

To-Do List

* **Think of your reputation as a brand and protect it**. You've got the power to control who people think you are at the office. Use that power!

* **Study your habits**. Are any of them weird or off-putting? If so, commit to changing them. Anyway, it's only the small stuff!

* **Remember the small stuff**. The tiniest things can come to define you, so think before you stink up the kitchen with tuna noodle casserole. You might be remembered for that forever!

* **Come up with a "classic you" calling card**. Just a small, positive signature act or two will keep you in good graces around the office.

* **Clean up your online image**. This is one area where you definitely can control the information out there about you. Don't damage yourself with inebriated photos and embarrassing commentary.

LESSON 5
Talk the Talk

"I was wondering if you had a chance to look at Page Six today?"

—Daniel Meade, quizzing his young assistant Betty on whether she was up to date on the latest industry buzz, on Ugly Betty

Betty never claimed to be a fashion or beauty expert. But to her go-getter credit, that didn't stop her from quickly becoming a mini-expert on the subject and using it to her advantage. Take, for example, when *Mode* was about to lose the Fabia Cosmetics advertising account just after she started. Instead of idly watching the project go down the drain, Betty took initiative and studied up so she could "talk the talk" for a proposal that helped win the business for *Mode*. Everyone's jaw dropped when she spouted off her well-researched statistics and insights about the company to Fabia herself.

As any boss would tell you, the wisdom in this situation isn't that Betty had a great understanding of the cosmetics company; it's simply that she knew how to swiftly present herself as knowledgeable. For her, it was as easy as browsing a few Web pages—or glancing at a newspaper column such as Page Six—and building a report around that information. It was a very shrewd, yet simple, move that you can learn from. Becoming an in-the-know employee who can "talk the talk" can be as easy as incorporating a few new habits—grounded in building a solid news-reading routine—into your daily schedule.

Become a News-Reading Geek

The most important step toward "talking the talk" around the office and coming off as an insider is to voraciously read every scrap of news you can find, especially that which concerns your industry. The following are suggestions about how to make the most of your daily news consumption.

Read the standard news every day. If you don't already, pick up a daily newspaper. Or, if that doesn't work for you, read the online edition of the *The New York Times*, or whatever big-city metro paper is near you, or even CNN.com. Just make sure that you're reading a good mixture of national and local news, as well as op-eds, that'll keep you up to date on current events and debates floating around your workplace's watercooler.

Become an industry news expert. A second part of your daily news routine should be gobbling up all the news about your industry that you can find. More than likely, there's a trade newsletter or possibly even some sort of daily dispatch, whether it goes out in a printed form or as an email newsletter. Some larger industries, such as finance, even have entire consumer papers, such as *The Wall Street Journal*, dedicated to them.

One of the first things I do every morning is read the online edition of the *Hollywood Reporter* and *Variety* because all the big entertainment news they break will undoubtedly be discussed at the morning staff meeting. If you don't know what your industry's daily news source is, just ask a coworker. Or, glance at their desk—the publication will likely be lying prominently on top of everything else.

"Keeping up with the industry and keeping up with current affairs is very important," says David Robinson, a senior lecturer in marketing at Berkeley's Haas School of Business. "Lots of young professionals don't do that; they don't keep up with current affairs at all, which only makes them seem ignorant around the office."

Subscribe to free email newsletters. Most news sources have free email newsletters that are essential, especially if they send out breaking news blasts. Even if you don't have time to read them as they come in to your in-box, save them in a folder and read them at the end of each week so you don't miss any information that could affect a project you're working on.

Obsess over that snarky industry blog. The magazine and media industries have Jezebel and Gawker, the tech industry has Valleywag, the Washington, D.C., political world has Wonkette, just to name a few. It's likely that your industry, too, has a snarky, rumor-filled blog that you should have bookmarked so you'll know the daily underground buzz. Kenny, a 25-year-old with a tech job in Silicon Valley, reads Valleywag every day and says it's "valuable because it provides the latest rumors circulating in the tech industry." Believing everything on such gossip-filled blogs is a different story, but people in your office will undoubtedly be talking about the latest posts, especially if they hit close to home.

Set Google News Alerts. This is honestly the easiest way to keep up to date on things you care about most. First, think about what keywords, companies, concepts, or people in your industry you want to be in the know about, then go to news.google.com and click on "News Alerts" to set up a direct email feed. Depending on how often you select to receive them, Google will send you an email when a news story with your keywords crosses their wire. If your boss or coworkers are industry movers and shakers, it's smart to put an Alert out for them too. If a story goes up about them, you'll be one of the first to know. Heck, I even have a Google News Alert set for myself. As a journalist, it's invaluable to see when my stories go up on EW.com and if any other outlets or blogs have picked up what I've written.

Troll other industry websites. Besides industry-centric blogs, find other websites that concern your profession and make sure to surf them once in a while. You never know what gem of an idea might be sparked by something on one of them. Editor-in-chief Deborah Ohrn says her employees with the best ideas get them "from interesting blogs. They're just always out there trolling in the evenings and bring in those awesome ideas in the morning. Employees who do this regularly are really valuable to me."

Showcase Your Smarts Every Day

Knowing about the big mergers or cutting-edge technology in your world will instantly raise your savvy quotient around the office. But don't just bottle that info up and do nothing with it: Use it to impress your boss and other coworkers.

Lexi, a 27-year-old editor in Massachusetts, offers this advice: "Never go into the office without having something smart to say about your industry that week. Even if you overlook 99 percent of the headlines your Google Reader picks up about your company or job field, read—and consider what your opinion actually *is* about—at least one or two news items before you enter any meeting. Smart, timely comments may go unnoticed, but lame, month-old musings can hurt you."

On the Job
• • • • •

Scenario: Finally! You scored what you think is sort of a dream job: doing publicity. The only catch is that you're into big-budget, blockbuster-type movies and this job is publicizing small art-house and indie films for a tiny production house. A few weeks into the job you realize you know absolutely nothing about the market. What to do?

✳

Quick Fix: Study up! Spend a weekend at a small theater watching everything they're showing, and possibly even invest in a Netflix account so you can catch up on old indie titles. Most importantly, be proactive! If you want to "talk the talk," you've just gotta do your research.

Real-Life "Betty"

"To keep up to date with patient literature, I read what they read. I try to frequently check out CNN Health. Dr. Gott has a national column where all kinds of people write in and ask health-related questions. I read that religiously because it never fails that my patients—I'm a pharmacist—will be asking for whatever miracle cure he's endorsing. Pharmacy and healthcare in general is always changing, so staying on top of current literature and guidelines is vital—not only hardcore medical literature—because it's essential to know what the general public is reading or listening to."

—Sara, 25, Sioux City, Iowa

• • • • • •

To-Do List

* **Learn the lingo**. Even if you just pick up a few basic business-related phrases, you'll be better off, but if you can learn your industry's lingo, you're on your way to success.

* **Study competitors**. Google them! Gather their annual reports! Subscribe to their publications! Honestly, it's such a great way to have a leg up.

* **Bookmark that snarky industry blog**. And refresh often! The rumors may not be true, but everyone in your office will definitely be talking about the posts.

* **Read a newspaper every day**. Or read a straight online news website. Smart people know about current events.

* **Do your research**. If you don't know something, look it up. Google every person you meet with and any client you're working with.

* **Obsess over industry news**. Subscribe to your industry's trade publications and email newsletters. Set Google Alerts for relevant terms. Troll the Internet for underground, insider-y information.

* **Always have something smart to say**. Don't leave home without one or two good opinions about something in your industry.

Part Two

Build Relationships

LESSON 6
Mind Your Boss

"Tell you what: I will try you out for a couple weeks, see if it works. If I don't like you, I'll fire you. If you don't like me, I'll fire you."

—*The Grinchy Lou Grant, upon hiring Mary Richards as an associate producer at WJM-TV in Minneapolis, on* The Mary Tyler Moore Show

Just like when Betty first met her boss Daniel Meade, another favorite pop culture working girl, Mary Richards of *The Mary Tyler Moore Show*, encountered a challenging boss in news director Lou Grant. Despite all his ranting about coworker Ted Baxter and his signature huffy, closed-door meetings, it became pretty clear by the end of the pair's seven seasons together that Lou was more bark than actual bite. To her credit, Mary figured that out and gave him exactly what he wanted in an employee: She continually strove to merge their working styles, which experts and young professionals advise is the first step toward building a good relationship with your boss.

The truth of the matter is that your boss is the second most important person to your career, behind yourself. It's scary, but your supervisor can make you or break you. Heck, even most senior-level bosses have someone they report to. The Donald Trumps and Bill Gates of the world, who rule their empires and answer to no one, are few and far between. So while you're waiting to rise to the level of Trump, focus on establishing a good relationship with your boss and work together to help each other get where you need to go.

Suss Out Your Boss's Working Style

One of the most important reasons why Mary Richards and Betty Suarez became professional successes was because of their strong relationships with superiors. To start with, they each determined what their boss's working style was and figured out how they fit into *his* equation. Even back when the doctors of *Grey's Anatomy* were interns, they wisely figured out how to work with barking resident Dr. Miranda Bailey, which was no easy feat.

Any working person should be focused on figuring out their boss, according to business professor David Robinson. "I think first it's important to realize that every boss has a different style," he says. "Some bosses like to be involved in every decision. Other bosses don't want to be bothered about almost anything. You have to diagnose your boss and his or her game, so you can play the game the way he or she wants. But, at the same time, you've got to retain enough of your own style so you don't end up in a place where you can't reasonably stand up to your boss, if need be."

Look for the clues as to your boss's style from the first time you meet: Does he prefer to communicate via email, on the phone, or in person? How does she treat her other direct reports? What's his temper like? Does she yell on a regular basis? Take note of how your coworkers act around your boss for a clear picture of his effect on employees. Robinson says that how the rest of the staff act tells you a lot about the boss. "I know a boss at a big firm who's known as a screamer. If anything is wrong, it's somebody's fault and he will make it very loud and very clear in front of other people," he says. "As a consequence, everybody who wants to get ahead in that company, even at the lowest levels, screams and shouts at one another, so they can compete with him."

It's smart to realize that, at least initially, you and your boss likely will have different working styles. "When you run into people where you're not connecting that doesn't mean you're right and they're wrong," says career counselor Dan King. "That just means you have some very different styles, and guess what? You're gonna run into a lot of that. So the question is, how can you balance that? How do you understand when your own personal style is working for you and when, frankly, it's just getting in the way?"

Communicate, Communicate, Communicate

It's simple, but oh-so-important advice: From day one on the job, you should be striving to make sure lines of communication are open with your boss. Along with figuring out your boss's working style, what's the best way to communicate? What are her expectations? Are you doing what you're supposed to be doing?

Says King: "Your best bet is to go in early and often to find out what they need. What are the problems they need solved? What do they need to see accomplished in the first 90 days? What are some of the issues that the company is facing? How does your role fit in the grander picture of what the company is doing? You need to be asking a lot of questions." And, ultimately, your boss should be asking you lots of questions too.

Things can get murky, of course, if you're unfortunate enough to have a boss who doesn't like to communicate. Joah, the 25-year-old consultant in Washington, D.C., who we met in lesson 3, learned the hard way. After a few weeks at an internship, he and his boss "got to the point of barely talking," he says. "She simply emailed me assignments and I kicked them out in time so that I wouldn't have to deal with her."

Ultimately, the pair "realized this was not a beneficial situation, either for the office or for my internship experience. We sat down and had a candid talk. From there, we identified some of my areas of improvement and some of the assignments that I enjoyed and wanted more of. In the end, I got a lot of good portfolio pieces over the summer and didn't leave with such a bad impression."

Your Boss Is Not Your Friend

While the line of professionalism may be foggy in other areas, when it comes to your relationship with your boss, it's rather clear: You are not friends outside of work. You may consider some of your coworkers to be friends, but, as tempting as it might be, slotting your boss into that category as well is just setting you up for workplace woes.

Elizabeth, a 26-year-old in sales in New York City, made the mistake of becoming too close to her boss. "When I moved to New York City, the girl I worked with in D.C. became my boss. We were coworkers and friends there, and since I didn't know many people in NYC, she became one of my regular friends," she says. "Between 40 to 60 hours a week at work, dinner some weeknights, and going out to brunch on the weekends, we became 24/7 besties. Since she was my boss, confidant, and job reference, she had so much power over my life, and I had a hard time standing up to her. And shocker: Once we both got new jobs, our friendship fell apart."

On the Job

• • • • •

Scenario: After months of managing a big project at your publicity job on your own, you've run into some major trouble. Sponsors have pulled out of the event you're working on and the client is annoyed. How do you tell your boss?

✳

Quick Fix: Regardless of your boss's working style, be honest in this situation. You could really use his expertise and help at this point, so it's best to just lay out the situation and see how the two of you can come up with a solution together. In the future, try to communicate about the status of your projects with your boss on a more frequent basis to avoid such an unfortunate situation.

Real-Life "Betty"

"I've got a terrible, tyrannical boss. Her mood is different by the minute, I'm constantly unsure if she's going to blow her top or be overly friendly, and she provides me with little feedback. In my next position, I will be very intentional about asking questions of my potential supervisor: What style do you have? Do you value team work? How do you support professionals? Plus, lots more. I've found support outside my immediate office, but I just had to seek it out. If anything, this experience has taught me how *not* to supervise. Currently, I only supervise one graduate student, but in the future, I will likely supervise an entire staff, like she does, and I now know how not to treat people who are a part of a team I depend on."

—*Christie, 27, Florida*

• • • • • •

To-Do List

* **Figure out your boss's working style**. The most important piece of advice to building a strong relationship: Once you determine his or her style, mimic away!

* **Remember your boss's pet peeve**. Be it long emails or overly hot coffee. Do not forget it.

* **Delineate exactly what your boss needs**. Fulfill those needs head over feet.

* **Help your boss shine**. You shine when he or she shines.

* **Communicate!** Have a regular system in place that works for the both of you about checking in, whether that be a daily meeting, daily email, weekly status report, or monthly lunch.

* **Know your authority and stay within it**. Usurping the parameters your boss has set is bad business.

* **Be punctual and don't waste your boss's valuable time**. This goes for anyone who's your superior.

* **Don't dump problems on your boss**. Instead, present the issue and your proposed solution.

* **Don't go over your boss's head**. Respect the communication channels set by your boss.

* **Be loyal and sincere**. You shall be rewarded.

* **Don't be friends with your boss**. It just gets awkward and you won't be able to stand up to your boss should you need to.

Discern Friends from Frenemies

"Look, you are one of us now, Betty. The Assistants Club! We have to protect each other."

—*Amanda Tanen, coercing Betty Suarez into lying about leaking a* Mode *secret, on* Ugly Betty

The social scene at any new job is just as scary as the first day of freshman year. But just comfort yourself with Betty's plight at *Mode*: There's little chance you'll have such scheming colleagues as her fellow assistants Amanda and Marc. To the resounding applause of career experts everywhere, Betty managed to build a working relationship with the pair, despite their sometimes dubious ulterior motives.

In any work situation, there are going to be coworkers that you see eye to eye with and ones you don't. Finding a handful of colleagues who are like-minded and can serve as confidants is the first step toward building a network. In Betty's case, she found a touchstone in fashion closet seamstress

Christina McKinney, who quickly became her go-to person at the office. Dealing with coworkers, however, is more complex than making a lunch buddy. Despite how close you may become, at the end of the day your colleagues are still *just* your coworkers, not your real friends. Plus, they're competition. So how do you deal? Find out.

Designate a Touchstone or Two

For the first month or so in a new workplace, you should focus on getting to know a little bit about a lot of people. Discern who you think you could bond with. The fact is that, for a good while, you will be spending a large portion of your days with these people, so it's smart to try to get along. When you're introduced around the office, remember who seems friendly and could potentially be a touchstone for you.

Editor-in-chief Deborah Ohrn is a huge proponent of employees building solid relationships at work. "You definitely need somebody who you can just share the daily dramas with. It's just asking: What does this mean? Or, how do I react?" she says. "It doesn't really go anywhere, but just so that you can feel better about what might be going on around you. And remember: This isn't gossiping. It's an effort to try to understand what's happening at work. It's gotta be someone you trust and it should be mutual sharing. I think that's a huge survival technique."

On *Grey's Anatomy*, most of the main characters are good friends and rely on each other to help them get through the hard times at Seattle Grace. Christina even calls Meredith her "person" because of how important she is for her to get through the day. Granted, while the interns-cum-doctors on *Grey's* may have taken their friendship to a rather inappropriate level at times, it's the same idea. They always were able to go to the bar together after a hard day at work to blow off steam or commiserate in the on-call room over patients who were especially hard to deal with.

That's exactly the case with Bridget Nelson, a 23-year-old research editor in New York City. "It's not like we all see each other or work together enough to be best friends or anything like that, but it's so nice to have other people who are somewhat new to the industry at work," she says. "The older employees are pretty sage, which is great when you need help or advice...but sometimes you just want to dish with someone and be like, 'I'm so stressed out' or 'What's up with that?' My coworkers and I use the on-site gym, go out to lunch every few weeks, signed up for a corporate 5K, and we even went to a comedy club in the city once...basically, little things that break up the normal workday routine."

Ohrn adds that "you definitely need that touchstone colleague, someone who is on your level." From her own experience, you shouldn't be sharing the daily dramas, which can be rather petty, with your boss, or vice versa. "Sometimes, occasionally, I've had to apologize to my staff because

I was bitching about my boss," she adds. "I shouldn't do that! They can't help me out, and it makes them feel awkward. I just need to share that with a colleague from another department."

But Remember: You're Paid to Play Nice with Coworkers

At the same time as you're making friends at work, you have to remember that these aren't your *real* friends. Despite all the good times I've had with the great people I've met at my three post-collegiate jobs, I only keep in touch with a select few of them on a personal level. For sure, I'd call many of my old colleagues professional contacts now, but that still doesn't mean I'd call them to spill my guts about my latest relationship problems.

Lindsay, a 25-year-old who started as a paralegal in New York City, says it's best to know the difference between work friends and real friends. "I think it's easy to confuse an office friend for a real friend. Some people are both office friends and real friends, but some friendships only happen nine to five and it's important to learn to distinguish the two," she says. "The problem is office friends care about the positive details of your life, whereas real friends are OK getting caught up in your personal drama. No matter where you start, even if it's in a job that's not your career, you never know where these people are going to pop up in your life, like in future jobs. So before you start spilling all your deepest secrets, I think it's important to wait to see what kind of friendship you have."

Competition Can Be a Good Thing

In sports, competition inspires athletes to go faster, throw farther, and kick harder. The same can be true in a work setting. No one wants to be upstaged. So with the coworkers you befriend and repel, a certain level of competition is bound to develop, especially if you're competing for projects or promotions.

"Regarding competition, I think it can be healthy to a certain degree," says Kenny, a 25-year-old working in the Silicon Valley tech industry. "But if you allow competition to bring you down, there is no way you will be able to focus on doing your job well in order to succeed. I've seen people affected negatively by competition, and they seem to become bitter employees who hate going into work every day. Managers see this and know that those people can't be depended on anymore."

Career counselor Dan King warns that competitiveness amongst coworkers does have its risks. "I think there's always a sense of competitiveness with your coworkers," he says. "If that competitiveness becomes 'I will do anything to win over them,' that's not healthy. You need to find common ground with others. You need to look for ways to create win-wins. You need to keep it professional at all times. For example, you might find in a meeting one of your coworkers offers an idea and you don't think it's a particularly good idea. If you turn around and respond with something like, 'Well, no I wouldn't do that, what I would do is this,' you've just created a faux pas there. You have shown that you will make that person look bad in order to make yourself look good. The way to handle it when somebody says something you don't agree with or that you don't think is a good idea, is to respond just by saying, 'That's a really good point, and I might look at it this way, as well.' What you've shown is that you're not going to step on that person to get ahead. You're going to preserve his dignity in the process, but you're still going to get your point out there. Those little habits can make such a difference. People sometimes think, Here's my chance to really get a good one in here, and the minute you start feeling competitive and use that to make the other person look bad, you're hurting yourself too."

On the Job
• • • • •

Scenario: Your nasty coworker seems out to get you. Whenever possible, he does something to make you look bad. What's the best plan of action in a situation like this?

✳

Quick Fix: Start by pulling the coworker aside to ask about the troubling actions. Be matter-of-fact instead of accusatory, and don't let your emotions get the best of you. Explain your side of the story, which might clear the air and solve the issue. If nothing else, it puts the coworker on notice that you won't allow this to continue. If that doesn't work, then document the behavior and approach your boss about your coworker impeding your productivity.

Real-Life "Betty"

"A colleague that I regularly associated with didn't just look at the world with a 'glass half empty' mentality. To her, the glass was chipped, there was no ice, and she didn't even want a glass with water in it in the first place. Nothing pleased her. A few months in, I started to really despise a lot of elements of my job: My boss was driving me crazy, my workload felt daunting, and my entire regard for our company was diminishing on a daily basis.

"But I discovered it was this coworker bringing me down. I could feel myself sinking to her level of unhappiness and it felt awful. I had to take swift action and quietly distanced myself from her. I thought it'd be hard at first because we work in a small office, but slowly and surely our lunch dates dwindled and our daily interaction did too. It was kind of awkward at first, but my attitude immediately began to turn around. I couldn't control her toxic attitude, but I sure as hell could control whether I spent time with her."

—Andrea, 25, Minneapolis

• • • • • •

To-Do List

* **Keep it friendly**. You want coworkers to like you, so try to make nice from the beginning.

* **Find a go-to person (or two)**. Have someone who you can bitch with after work, where the conversation will go no further.

* **Know that your work friends are not your real friends**. Keep it professional. Most industries are very small, and you are likely to encounter the same people in future jobs.

* **Be nice, but competitive**. Being competitive keeps you sharp.

* **Avoid toxic coworkers**. They'll only serve to bring you down, so it's best to just stay away, if possible.

Don't Ignore Office Politics

"Don't be afraid of office politics. Do favors for the right people. You just might get rewarded at the end. Unfortunately, that is the cruel reality in this business."

—*Wilhelmina Slater, enticing fashion closet seamstress/ wannabe designer Christina McKinney to go along with her evil scheme, on* Ugly Betty

As unsavory as they may seem, office politics are an unfortunate reality in nearly every work setting. You can count on bosses favoring certain employees over others, projects that seem predicated on bad ideas being pushed through inexplicably, and old guard employees undoubtedly battling to the death with the new. Despite your insistence that it won't affect you, keep on dreaming.

At *Mode*, a major political undercurrent has brewed since even before Betty began: Diabolical creative director Wilhelmina has been on the warpath to take down the Daniel Meade regime and install herself as editor-in-chief. In the passage above, Wilhelmina is enticing fashion closet maven Christina to do her bidding. Try as she might, Christina wasn't able to stay neutral, and against what I'd advise any young professional, she got involved by keeping secrets, scheming, and even breaking into Wilhelmina's apartment! Let's hope it doesn't go that far in your case, but it can't hurt to know a thing or two about how to handle the sticky situations that will surely come your way.

You Can't Change the Politics, so Figure Out How to Deal with Them

Politics. "The word is a dangerous word," says career counselor Dan King. "When we think politics, I mean in the greater sense, there's not a positive that most of us have about it." And you should be leery, but not scared. It's typical to roll into your first professional gig wide-eyed and thinking that you can stay safe by just ignoring office politics. If it were only that easy! Despite your attempts to act like they don't exist, the politics of your office are bound to have an effect on the job you do. But that effect doesn't have to be negative, if you're smart.

Instead of getting involved in your office's nasty web of politics, the smartest move is to just understand what the undercurrents are so you know what and whom to avoid. "A lot of twentysomethings sort of scoff at politics and say, 'Well, I'm just not going to play,'" says King. "Well, that's akin to taking the ball and going home. You may not want to play the politics, but that doesn't mean they're going to go away. They're still there. So how are you going to navigate those? What are you going to do? And for most of us, when we say I don't want to play, what we mean is, 'I don't want to sacrifice my integrity or lose my soul in the process here. I want to remain true to myself.'"

After you identify the potential land mines that are buried deep into the history of your office, make like a cautious soldier and skedaddle! In other words, don't be the one to trigger an explosion. "My advice would be to be aware of the land mines and tiptoe through and avoid them," says business professor David Robinson. "But there are some people who actually like to go around exploding the land mines. Some people like playing the game."

I'd never advise you to "play the game," but I would tell you to know what game is going on around you. What really floors superiors in your office? What kind of people seem to get promoted? What are taboo conversations? Figuring out things like these are essential to your success.

Stay in Your Own Movie

A boss of mine once passed along this advice whenever petty fights erupted around the office: "Stay in your own movie." What on earth did she mean? If you think about your job as a movie—or, more appropriately in this framework, a television show—don't make a point to jump into someone else's storyline that may just get you mired in muck you didn't even know existed.

"In most cases, getting involved in whatever mess is going on will only bring you down," says editor-in-chief Deborah Ohrn. "I can remember the reputation of one person who didn't even work in my group. Around the office it became, 'Yeah, she's a gossip.'"

Elizabeth, a 26-year-old in sales in New York City, has dealt with her share of interoffice drama. Her advice? Stay away! "Don't take sides," she says. "When there's drama between two coworkers, as I experienced, you definitely do not want to take sides. Office politics can definitely work for or against you, but try to avoid them as much as possible."

Pick Your Battles

All of this advice about avoiding politics probably sounds pretty rosy, right? Just avoid any political issues that come your way? Not so fast: The fact of the matter is that you'll probably have no choice but to step into some unsavory drama from time to time. So when you do, make sure that it's about an issue, a project, or a coworker that you care enough about to fight for. There's no sense in putting your neck on the line just for the sake of ruffling feathers.

There are times where diving in and making a splash can be worth it. But choose those situations wisely or you may just be seen as a creator of drama. "People see politics as a tool for people who can't get ahead on merit," says King. "Well, guess what? You can't get ahead on merit alone. If you think of them as a source of personal power—and power not being a negative word here—and if you can learn to navigate the politics and build some network of influence throughout the organization, you are able to get a lot of things that you want done."

On the Job
• • • • •

Scenario: You're a loyal, hard-working employee, but your boss plays favorites and seems to pass the plum assignments on to a particular coworker. The reason likely has to do with office politics. What should you do?

✳

Quick Fix: To begin with, you shouldn't just assume that you're a victim of favoritism. Before crying foul and making an unpleasant situation even worse, communicate to your supervisor that you're interested in taking on additional responsibility. This just could be a case where your manager doesn't know that you're ready for more to do, or your boss could be waiting for you to step up and show initiative. Keep it professional and don't point fingers. If you've clearly expressed your aspirations, you should ask about the specific steps to landing higher-profile assignments. Keep the conversation positive by focusing on your desire to grow and improve, not your frustration. Expressing a "sour grapes" mentality will only work against you.

Real-Life "Betty"

"Office politics can be very tricky. For example, the company I previously worked for heavily favored the interns from the previous summer who were coming on full-time. Not only did they get to choose their start dates before the other new hires, but they also received a bigger signing bonus and had tenure over everyone else in their class. In addition, the partners in the firm often would choose them for their cases over any other new hire. This caused resentment among the rest of the new hires.

"As a non-intern new hire, I had to be careful when pushing for a particular case I wanted because, due to this political situation, there was a fine line between going after what you wanted and annoying the staffing manager or partners. Basically, as a new hire, I had to be careful about whose toes I was stepping on every day. Piss off someone more senior than me, and I'd end up blacklisted by everyone."

—Kenny, 25, Silicon Valley, California

• • • • • •

To-Do List

* **Have a clear agenda**. Be transparent, but not invisible, about what you're doing and you're less likely to incense your coworkers.

* **Be flexible**. Your rigid attitude will only get others riled up unnecessarily.

* **Fight for what's important**. If you really don't care about it, without question, let it go.

* **Watch out for those land mines**. Once you know where the power struggles are, or who likes to cause trouble, you can head in the opposite direction.

* **Get rid of your ego**. When your ego is involved, you and your work suffer. Fighting over who's right just for the sake of winning never helped get a project finished.

* **Lose the idea of "territory."** Let others in. That's the surest way to show them that you're not political when it comes to who gets to do what.

* **Avoid gossip**. Plain and simple, it's tacky. And just think about how you look at people who you discover unnecessarily gossip and spread rumors around.

* **Focus**. What's the business issue you're dealing with? Don't get swallowed up in the power struggles and other politicking.

LESSON 9

Be Wary of Office Romance

"Did you let me scrub in for this operation because I slept with you?"

—Meredith Grey, questioning how her relationship with Dr. Derek Shepherd may be dubiously benefiting her at work, on Grey's Anatomy

Without question, romance is especially sticky when it plays out in a professional setting. Television shows featuring young professionals have proved that point with a dramatic exclamation point. Take the romantic pursuits of the crew of young doctors on *Grey's Anatomy*, for example. Meredith dates Derek off and on; Christina lived with Dr. Burke for a couple seasons and the pair nearly married; and Callie married George, who then dumped her for Izzie.

Although much of what happens between these couples is done to pump up the drama on the show, their break-ups, hookups, and ensuing problems ultimately affect the workplace dynamic, usually in a negative way. The quote from Meredith above—her questioning whether she got a leg up simply because she hooked up with a higher-up—-

illustrates the murky nature of dating a coworker or, as in this case, a superior.

The best advice is to skip the *Grey's Anatomy* route and simply avoid romantic dalliances at work. But let's face it: Sometimes love strikes in the most inopportune places at the most inopportune times. Before sinking your teeth into an office fling, however, consider a few factors.

Think Before Leaping

The chances of meeting someone you're at least interested in at work are relatively good. Career counselor Dan King has seen it happen time and time again. "When you think about how much we're all at work and the statistics of where you're going to meet somebody, it's likely that it'll be at the office," he says. "Most of the people you meet in the course of the day are gonna be at work." But, to that point, he also adds, "The whole area of office romance is tricky."

First things first, you should check to see if your company has a policy on coworkers dating. Although it's never addressed on *Ugly Betty*, Henry and Betty should have done this before they struck up their love connection, though luckily it hasn't really affected their careers so far. "A lot of organizations have strict policies against workplace romance and you need to know where your organization stands on that," King adds. "Generally, there is a policy. They may not have one, but when it comes up, there's one that gets created."

Let's say you think you really might like someone in the office and it's allowed. That's fine and all at face value, but first think about what a romance with someone in the office could do to the career you've worked so hard to achieve. When Angela and Dwight broke up on *The Office*, any interaction between the couple at work became awkward and forced—even more so than before. They could barely work together.

Wondering about the ramifications of workplace romance? There are a few sticking points to think about:

Colleague fallout. Especially if you're dating your boss, which is pretty much always a no-no, coworkers likely won't have much tolerance for your romance. No matter how competent you are, the perception will be that your relationship is fueling your career, especially if you're receiving promotions or given the corner office. Even the simplest things can seem like favoritism.

Your career in jeopardy. If you break up with your boss, or even just a coworker, think about how miserable you could be every day. *Ugly Betty* assistant Amanda made the wrong move of getting involved with editor-in-chief Daniel and it was a detriment to her working relationship with him after things ended nastily. While it's totally unprofessional, your brokenhearted ex could find numerous ways to make your workday unbearable or even jeopardize your success within the company. Would you be willing to leave your job if the situation became too uncomfortable after the breakup? That's certainly something to think about.

The (nearly inevitable) breakup. While it may seem preemptive to think about the end before a relationship even begins, this is definitely a concern because breakups tend to be rough for even the strongest of people. The best thing about most romances, though, is that once you've moved on from the person, you typically never have to see your ex again. That's obviously not the case in an office or other workplace, where you'll likely still have to face the former flame on a daily basis.

Outline Some Ground Rules

Simply keeping your behavior in check at work can stop many of the concerns that will arise from a workplace romance. Here are four steps to doing just that:

1. **Stay professional**. Just heed this as your golden rule: When you are in the office, you are coworkers *and* professionals. Treat your boyfriend or girlfriend just as you would anyone else. Candace, a 24-year-old in the New York City real estate industry, had an office relationship and smartly kept it professional at work so colleagues wouldn't have ammunition against either of them. "I've always felt that colleagues knowing per-

sonal information about me gives them leverage and power," she says. "There are certain things they don't need to know, especially the higher up they are."

2. **Nix public displays of affection**. Nothing makes people more uncomfortable than seeing coworkers smooching, so keep it under wraps until you're off company property or away from a company-sponsored event.

3. **Keep nonbusiness-related communication to a minimum**. Time spent flirting or sending email back and forth will only be scrutinized more closely when you're dating a coworker. You might have been able to get away with it more before the cat was out of the bag, but it'll only be more obvious, and annoying, to those around you when it's clear you're dating.

4. **Discuss the breakup**. Just have a plan of action ready in case you do break up. Of course, no one wants to talk about a breakup that may never happen, but it's a necessary evil if you're dating a coworker.

Disclose the Romance when Necessary

If for nothing else than to extinguish office rumors that may be flying around, figure out when and how is the best time to disclose your relationship to your coworkers. If it gets to the point of marriage, it's not a question of whether or not the brass *needs* to know—you have to tell them. It's not a law, but it's a necessary professional courtesy. Let's just say that if your bosses find out on their own accord—especially if the relationship is disrupting the office atmosphere—you will be one unhappy, and possibly fired, employee.

"You have to assess your situation and you have to look at the culture to decide what to do," says King. "You have to get clear on where you stand and what you're willing to accept as far as a policy that comes down on it."

In fact, King knows firsthand about how relationships can affect your job. "When I met my wife, we were working together," he says. "We had it kept under wraps for a long time, but when it did come out, it was an explosive situation that in hindsight we probably could have done a little more groundwork to make it not so bad. It blew up and it was like, 'Okay, one of us has to leave.' Then there were, of course, all the water-cooler stories: 'Did you hear what happened?' and so on. What complicated it was that I was a manager and she wasn't, so that made it even worse because of the possibility of favoritism."

On the Job
• • • • •

Scenario: Despite your best efforts to keep your office romance on the down-low, the truth is out there now and you're afraid of the repercussions that could be coming from your bosses or coworkers. How do you handle this romantic quandary gracefully?

✳

Quick Fix: First, if you haven't already, check out the official line from the company on romances. More than likely, it just will apply to couples who are married, but it can't hurt to check. Then, if needed, look at your behavior and modify it. Were you and your new boyfriend or girlfriend running off together at lunch? Flirting near the bathrooms at all times of the day? That kind of behavior isn't office appropriate and is inconsiderate to others around you. Finally, you may want to just let your boss know. Depending on what kind of boss you have, she may have already realized what's going on, but it can't hurt to just put the information out there. Who knows, she may even have some words of wisdom for you.

Real-Life "Betty"

"It all started during a school assembly. I was a new teacher in a new school and town. This female teacher had been teaching for a couple of years. We eyed each other as the principal was telling the students to sit down. Since I'm a nice Southern gentleman and she was an attractive female, I began the small talk. She asked me to come to her room after school to make plans for the football game that night. Since we are adults, we went to Chili's before the game [and had some drinks]. However, my new 'friend' became a little over-served. This was my first sign of impending doom. But the game went great, and on the way back to the car, she invited me back to her place. I was forced to decline the offer. I now try to keep my distance from her. Relationships scare me in general, but a relationship with a coworker scares me even more."

—John, 28, Nashville

• • • • • •

To-Do List

* **Examine your company's policy on workplace romance**. It likely will shed light on what you may be required to reveal, per your company.

* **Consider the consequences**. A romance between coworkers—or the much more sticky, and totally

ill-advised, situation between a boss and an employee—will definitely change the dynamics of your career and other office relationships.

* **'Fess up**. It's silly to try and hide an office romance. You're likely not duping anyone. When the time is right, let your coworkers know, but don't make a big deal out of it.

* **Set some ground rules**. It's super important that you and your new lover behave professionally at work. Decide what's appropriate and what won't make your officemates uncomfortable.

* **Nix the public displays of affection**. Don't get physical at work and be discreet.

* **Date on your level only**. Not all workplace romances are created equal, and dating the boss, or someone even more senior, will only put your intentions into question.

* **Break up gently**. If your relationship goes kaput, try to maintain some semblance of a friendship with the person; otherwise, you may be in for some painful days at work.

Know the People Who *Really* Make Things Happen

"Oh, Amanda! Gosh, you look so pretty today. I love that sweater.... Look, Daniel says you have access to theater tickets. Please! I'll do anything you want."

—*Betty Suarez, blatantly sucking up to receptionist-with-power Amanda for her theater tickets connection, on* Ugly Betty

Besides your bosses and coworkers, there are a few other key people in the workplace who are super important to your success. I'm talking about the office manager, the mailroom staff, the receptionist, the janitor, and so on. The list is really endless, and you may even be one of these people to someone else, especially if you're an assistant.

The example above may seem silly, but it does illustrate the power that many people in your office may have without your knowledge. In this case, snarky receptionist Amanda can get Broadway tickets for anyone in the office, but only if you're on her good side. Betty and Amanda have a rocky relationship at best, but with a few nice words and a promise to walk Amanda's dog for a month, Betty got what she wanted.

The wisdom here is that these are the relationships that can help you get things done when you're in bind. Need something taken to FedEx after hours? Good thing you're friends with the gals in the mailroom. Can't find enough binders for your boss's special report? You're lucky that the office manager likes you and has a secret stash he's willing to share.

Show Goodwill to the "Office Master"

Every office has one: the person who holds the cards when it comes to anything functional around the office. Let's call that person the "office master." He's the one who you can go to and ask any question for the scoop, the nitty gritty, the details. This person should be immediately on your radar when you start a new job. She'll likely be easy to find because her desk is typically a hub of activity.

Don't mess around. This is the person who'll likely get you into the office late at night when you forgot to do something. Or, he'll be the person who orders you those extra supplies you need in a pinch. Or, she'll take care of an important portion of your administrative duties when you're out of the office on vacation.

I'm thinking back to my first internship, during my sophomore year of college. The office manager was a cheerful, grandmotherly woman named Barb. Of course, my bosses had given me the quick tour and sat me down in my cube with a few assignments, but I still didn't really have a clue about what was actually going on around the office. It was Barb who held my hand, but she only did so because I was nice to her. I bugged her every few minutes about this or that. More than anything else, she filled me in on the lay of the land: Who was prickly and worth avoiding? Who was nice and worth going to chat with? How did I get paid? How do I get a check cut for a freelancer? Where are back issues of projects? Do we have a research library I can use? She became a good work friend over my three years in that office.

To get in their good graces, Harold Bell, director of career planning and development at Spelman College in Atlanta, stresses that it's just the little things that are the most important. "A lot of times, it's not about extensive kinds of things," he says. "It's just maybe remembering things they like. I remember I was filling out my parking form, and just in conversation with the parking attendant I found out she loved cranberry juice. So for her birthday, I brought her over some cranberry juice. What these people will do—once you find value in them—is things that could potentially be obstacles, they start removing them for you. A whole new world will open up to you."

A Breakdown of the Important Folk

You actually may be one of these important people without a glamorous title, so who should be bringing you plates of cookies? In Betty's case, she even learned the power of being friends with the office sandwich guy—a tactic that proved shrewd later when she needed his van to haul something to the office. Here's a rundown of the players:

The mailroom staff. Can't figure out how to mail that oversized poster or extremely delicate box of light bulbs? If the mailroom staff likes you, they'll definitely help. If not, you just might be dealing with an upset client come delivery.

The office manager. This is your go-to person for nearly everything. Supplies? Keys? Basic processes? You bet. The office manager even may be able to provide a little off-the-record gossip or details about how best to navigate the office.

The receptionists. They can harass your guests or let them into the office without a peep. Plus, they even may be willing to warn you when your boss is on the way in or out, which could be essential to your survival.

The assistants. Nearly anyone with assistant in their title is worth knowing. They usually keep their boss's schedules and may be privy to information that could be helpful to you.

The building manager. Looking for additional chairs or tables for an event you're putting on at work? This is the type of person who'd help you, but maybe only if you're on his good side.

The security guards. They are the people to know when you've left your building pass upstairs or need to get back into the building after hours. They can make it easy or hard, so it's worth giving them a smile every day to grease the wheels for those unfortunate days.

The janitors. Oops! You've got a big mess to clean up. You could be responsible for doing it yourself, or a quick call to your friend the janitor might mean you'd have an extra pair of hands to help out.

The tech people. They can make getting your computer fixed—thus keeping you working swiftly for your boss—quick and painless *or* long and arduous. I remember spilling a coffee all over my keyboard one day and feeling awful about it. But because I had a good relationship with one of the guys in IT, he replaced it with no questions asked.

On the Job
• • • • •

Scenario: Unfortunately, your boss requires you to be at your desk late into the evening to make sure you don't miss any of his phone calls while he's there. Many nights, you have to order his dinner too, but can't get up to get it when it's delivered. Who, pray tell, could help you with this situation?

✳

Quick Fix: The answer to this one is simple: Make friends with the receptionist! Or another assistant who isn't so chained to his or her desk. Then you either can have one of them sit in for you while you go grab the dinner or ask them kindly to pick it up for you. Of course, you'll owe them a favor, but at least you'll be pleasing your boss, which is most important.

Real-Life "Betty"

"I made friends with the janitor and the building manager. They make my life as a middle-school special education teacher so much easier! Seriously, I get so many perks that the other teachers don't get: The janitor hand delivers the paper to me every morning. She's totally awesome. Anytime something is broken in my room, they're the first people there. I had an unfortunate incident with a broken toilet in my classroom last year and they saved me. I've learned you really have to get in with the right people. That sounds self-serving, but really the relationship is mutually beneficial: I bring them coffee and let them in on the treats I bring for the class."

—*Jessica, 25, Denver*

• • • • • •

To-Do List

* **Find the value in every person in the office**. And then make sure you're in their good graces.

* **Know the "office master."** This person can be the key to your success—or stand between you and greatness.

* **Remember these people when you're in a position of power**. They were good to you, so remember to be good to them.

Part Three

Become Irreplaceable

LESSON 11
Go the Extra Mile

"No, I can't! Because that would make me a brownnoser, and everyone hates brownnosers. I cannot be a brownnoser."

—Christina Yang, waxing about being so on top of her game at work that she annoys her boss, on Grey's Anatomy

Betty Suarez's job as the assistant to the editor-in-chief of *Mode* magazine is typical of an entry-level position: long hours, menial tasks, a demanding boss, and a cutthroat environment that requires a load of gumption. The interns-turned-residents on *Grey's Anatomy* are in a similar situation, where they're constantly challenged to prove themselves as doctors who contribute wholeheartedly to the hospital. The Seattle Grace gaggle is pushed to their limits, and, despite all their personal dalliances at work, they still manage to go above and beyond in a spectacular fashion. In the quote above, Christina even admits that sometimes she goes too far—if that's even possible—in terms of being a standout. She's certainly an extreme case, but you can learn from her persistence and obsessive dedication to her work.

Simply put, that perseverance to constantly improving and taking on more responsibility is a huge part of the reason that all of these fictional young professionals are successes. The fact that they'll volunteer to scrub in for a last-minute, late-night surgery even though they've already been working all day, or will pull an all-nighter to pass their intern exams, is what makes them extra valuable to the chief at Seattle Grace.

And as for you and your career? The same applies. There's an old saying that says the early bird gets the worm. Well, when it comes to your career, the busybody employee gets the promotion.

Put Your Pride Aside and Say "Yes"

Especially when you begin your job, you'll undoubtedly be asked to do work that may seem beneath you: simple tasks like handling the office's billing or creating dozens of mind-numbing spreadsheets with facts and figures. Having been in similar situations many a time, I was offended at first and thought, You want me to do what? A monkey could do those things and that's not why I went to college for four years!

The best advice here is to take on those tasks and own them. Smile when they're assigned and do them with such panache that your boss will be forced to give you better projects in the future. Chad Macy, a regional managing director for staffing company Spherion in Austin, Texas, and regular blogger for spherioncareerblog.com, agrees. "You should just put all pride aside and do the grunt tasks, work as hard as you can, because that is going to create an image of you as a hard worker, someone who goes above and beyond," he says. "No one will ever question how hard you work."

Brad Karsh, the Chicago-based founder of jobbound. com and author of *Confessions of a Recruiting Director: The Insider's Guide to Landing Your First Job*, stresses the importance of being a team player, no matter what you're asked to do. "It's about having a great attitude when they're like, 'Hey, Phil, why don't you go make 50 copies for the meeting?' And you're like, 'I'd be happy to make 50 copies.'" he says. "Instead of scoffing and saying, 'How dare you! I went to four years of college to make copies?' It's doing, really, anything and everything."

Your coworkers who aren't doing that may look on you with frustration at times, especially if they're not working on raising the bar themselves. "You can't concern yourself with that," says Macy, who sees it as his job as a manager to reward those who are doing what's asked of them. "I view it as my job to compliment people around me and reward them for their successes as often as possible."

Take Initiative

Karsh cautions that your first job should not be viewed like the work you did in college. "In college, if you do what you're told and you do it well, you get an A," he says.

"If you answer every question correct on the test and get them all right, you get an A. In the working world, if you do what you're told and you do it well, you're barely going to pass."

What he's talking about is initiative. "More than anything else it's critical to your success in the working world. A lot of students, when they start their first job as a young professional—after working for six months—go to their boss, and say, 'Look, I've been doing everything you've asked me to do. Where's my raise? Where's my promotion?' And the boss is like, 'No, no, you don't understand. What I tell you to do is the barebones minimum to allow you to keep your job.'"

So what does that mean? How are you supposed to know what to do beyond your basic assigned tasks? Think beyond just taking tasks from point A to point B. Put on your thinking cap and see if you can't figure out a way to get to C and anticipate other problems of the project. "Going the extra mile is not just existing in your job and trying to survive, but studying what you need to know, learning how your job impacts other areas, and getting to know people in other departments that your job could interface with," says Macy. "It's truly about walking in and understanding what you're doing and creating a plan for yourself of what you want to achieve. And always be willing to, when your job is over, help others in theirs."

Initiative on your end can manifest itself in a variety of ways, whether it's doing an analysis of your competitors when no one asked you to or something as simple as pitching in wherever you can. For example, you just heard they're forming a group to take on a new project. What do you do? Throw your hat in the ring and tell your boss how happy you'd be to help out.

Macy also suggests you ask for additional assignments when your work is done. "Don't sit idly," he advises. "Don't wait until somebody gives you something else. Finish, and then ask for more. I've been a manager for over ten years now and my experience is that managers—and not just them, but people around you too—are more than happy to give something to somebody to get it off their plate, so it'll get done. It doesn't mean that's a high-level management task, but it could be something that gives you additional responsibility, makes you look good in front of others, and helps you in your progression. When you start to take on additional projects and show that you can multitask and handle more, more will continue to be given to you. Sometimes, you can walk yourself into another job or a promotion just for the pure fact that you're already starting to perform the work of the next step up or the next person."

Figure Out the Bigger Picture

Understanding how what you do fits into the bigger picture and strategy of your company also will allow you to do more. So simply put, ask how it does. You'll instantly be able to do a better job with your piece of the puzzle.

Karsh uses an anecdote to explain: "Say your boss says, 'Hey listen, I want you to research the past ten Oscar award winners for best picture.' You could be like, 'OK, I'll go do it,' or you could ask, 'Well, what's it for?' Your boss replies, 'We're doing this project on previous Oscar award winners and where the films are now.' Once you know that, you might think, Huh, where are they now? There was a great Oscar award winner 15 years ago and a where are they now story for it that could be even better than other things. What a great idea! So always finding out how it fits within the bigger picture helps you figure out in what capacity to display that initiative or to go that extra mile." In this situation, as in most, asking for more details is extremely appropriate and only will help both you and your boss produce the best work possible.

On the Job
· · · · ·

Scenario: You're bored at work. When you interviewed, your boss said you'd be able to really sink your teeth into high-profile projects, while also taking on a fair amount of administrative work to support the department. Unfortunately, most of what you've been doing seems menial. How can you get an opportunity to make more of a contribution to the real work around the office?

✳

Quick Fix: First off, it's good to hear you're such a go-getter! But the fact is that your boss may not realize the problem and, unfortunately, may even think you're just overwhelmed with the small tasks you've been given already. What kind of message are you sending? Have you let your boss know that you're ready for more? Or are you just giving off the vibe that making copies overwhelms you? Take a tad of initiative and let your boss know through direct and indirect cues that you're ready for more challenging tasks.

Real-Life "Betty"

"When I was 21 and in college, I held an internship where doing much of anything beyond what I was supposed to rarely crossed my mind. I was ambivalent. Though I recognized that I wasn't completely happy with what I was doing, I never thought to find something else that might've made me tick, something for which I was better suited. I wasn't making the internship one of my major priorities—I fell behind school, behind my own writing, behind sleep too. Consequently, things ground to a halt and I was let go. I'd disregarded an experience that could've been worthwhile, which was, of course, disappointing. Needless to say, I received my proverbial wake-up call; my work ethic improved. I went on to graduate school, where, at one point, I worked three jobs while attending to my academic and writerly responsibilities. Having recently finished graduate work, I'm now settling into my first nine-to-five, looking forward to what I'll accomplish in the future, and enjoying the newfound free time that my evenings and weekends have given me."

—*Shannon, 25, Seattle*

• • • • • •

To-Do List

* **Look for ways to take initiative**. Don't just do what's asked of you. Take it to the next level.

* **Pitch in wherever you can**. Volunteering to be a part of a team or take on an additional project shows you're a team player and makes you very valuable to your boss.

* **Be a "yes" employee**. Swallow your pride and take on whatever task you're assigned with a smile.

* **Ask for more work**. Bosses love to hand off projects to willing employees. When you've finished your assigned work, find out what else you might be able help with.

* **Understand the bigger picture**. Then it'll be easier to understand how your part of the project fits in. Ultimately, you'll be able to modify it if you have a better idea.

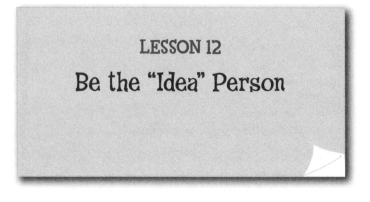

"Well, it was your whole blank slate thing that gave me the idea. Thank you very much. You know, Betty, you're really good at this."

—*Betty Suarez's boss Daniel Meade praising her for her inspired idea, on* Ugly Betty

The number of times Betty saved the day with her genius are too many to count. Whether it was pitching the winning idea for the Fabia Cosmetics account or even just showing smarts by suggesting a dazzling new photographer, having a creative streak serves Betty well. Once, she literally saved the day: Right after Bradford died, Wilhelmina crashed all the computers at *Mode* just before the magazine went to press. Before her bosses could even get back to the office to start damage control, Betty was there and had called in the entire staff, her first great idea and act of initiative. In fact, when the magazine needed a new cover later in the evening, she suggested a reshoot. And while that cover didn't work out in the end, it was a later discussion with her boss Daniel—illustrated by the quote above—that was the inspiration for what finally went on the front of the magazine. Idea after idea makes her a complete asset to her boss and the staff.

What is important about all this is Betty's constantly creative mind. Even if your ideas don't always work out, like Betty's cover reshoot that fell apart, they show your boss that you're thinking about how to improve and do your job better. Follow her example! Just like with Betty, your superiors will look to you for inspiration and that will undoubtedly set you apart from other employees.

Creativity Factors into All Careers

I hear it all the time from all kinds of people when the conversation turns to careers: "It must be so fun to have a creative job!" "Yes, it is," I respond. "I went into the magazine industry because I wanted to be creative on a daily basis." But they're shocked with what I tell them next: Every career is creative! Just listen for a minute. It may not be that you're literally putting words on a page like me or coming up with ideas about how you can package a television story, but if you're not thinking about your tasks in terms of creative problem solving, you're missing out on a great opportunity to wow your boss.

Creativity can manifest itself in so many ways: everything from how to improve an antiquated process to coming up with the advertising slogan that wins over a client. But, when you're young at work, it's probably best to think about it on a smaller scale. Within the projects you're working on, what can be improved? How can fresh ideas and perspective contribute to making what you're doing better? Is there a better accounting practice that'll save time and money? Has the company considered pitching the clients with this angle? It even may be something as simple as implementing a digital billing service that'll make your administrative duties easier.

The point is that you have the power to be creative—and wield your ideas—in any position, no matter how big or small. Being constantly creative and supplying those ideas will serve only to make you that much more irreplaceable to your boss.

Be a Creative Problem Solver

"Being an idea person is not being somebody who's constantly coming up with the most bizarre ideas and then being seen or viewed as a high-maintenance person," says Spherion's regional managing director, Chad Macy.

Career expert Brad Karsh adds: "It's not about being whacky creative; it's about being a creative problem solver. Ultimately, it goes to the whole notion of initiative. You should always be thinking: How can we do this faster? How can we do this better? How can we do this more cheaply? How can we do it more efficiently?"

Heed These Tips for Creativity

Looking to be the best problem solver in the office? Here are some golden rules of workplace creativity:

Examine what's closest to you. You immediately can make a difference with your creative ideas in this realm, especially with day-to-day tasks that you handle. As a new employee, you've got an invaluable fresh perspective. "Someone might say, 'Oh, we've been doing it this way for the past 73 years,'" says Karsh. "Well, you know, maybe that's not the best way to do it. Don't be afraid to make suggestions for improvement. As a new employee, you can walk in and say, 'Hey, I'm pretty involved in this invoice process that we do, and instead of sending it here, here, and here, if we sent it here right away, wouldn't that save us three steps?'"

Read widely. The best ideas are generated from what you read. According to Macy, soaking up as much information as possible from blogs to magazines to business journals makes you well-rounded and brimming with current, useable knowledge. For instance, if you read a case study or a profile about what a company similar to yours did to fix a problem with great success, think about how you could modify what they did and capitalize on that same success in your position.

Understand your organization's mission. Once you know, live, and breathe what your company's goals are, you'll be able to generate ideas that have great impact more often. "The thing that I see as lacking in a lot of young professionals is that they perform their task and then they check out without really thinking about who their world touches and how their job impacts other people," says Macy. "They need to start to look, at all times, for deficiencies and make sure that what they do propose jives with the company's mission."

Always have a fresh idea on hand. Especially when you head into a brainstorming session or any kind of meeting, arm yourself with a couple of ideas. You never know when you'll be called upon to offer up something, and goodness knows you don't want to be speechless when all eyes are on you. Additionally, this is where you really can shine with well-thought-out positions and ideas that wow your coworkers and superiors.

Offer solutions, not problems. "It's an expression that I love," Karsh says. "I didn't come up with it, but I wish I did. When you're talking to a coworker or a manager, don't go to them with problems, go to them with solutions." Creative people don't whine about the problems they're faced with, they do something about it! Trust me, your boss will thank you for offering solutions before crying about problems.

Get people on board with your ideas. Try introducing them in meetings or brainstorming sessions where ideas are openly welcomed. If you're serving up a good idea, coworkers will likely respond. "Introduce ideas in a public setting because the more people that can poke holes in your ideas, the better," says Macy. "Don't be afraid of looking like a fool—and just because your idea is shot down doesn't mean that you are. Throw it out there and say, 'I was looking at this and had a question. Can you all give me your opinion?' If you're presenting it in a way of soliciting opinions instead of saying, 'OK, we need to change this,' then people are more likely to buy in."

Realize not every idea will go through. "It's important to take the pride and emotion out of the ideas," says Macy. "You may look at something and think, We've always done it this way. Maybe they're doing it that way because they've always done it this way and it's not very efficient, but then there could be a business reason that you can't change because of your customer or because of your system or technology limitations that force you to do it in that way. So understand that if you offer a solution and be that idea person, that some of your ideas will have to be rejected."

On the Job
• • • • •

Scenario: You're the grunt on a consulting project, but you've got a stellar idea that really could take the project in an exciting direction. You have a daily status meeting where the head of the project genuinely seems to want feedback from all the players, and you've seen others on your level speak up. Do you propose your idea?

✳

Quick Fix: Hell yes! Like much of this chapter has talked about, present it in question fashion, such as, "I was thinking about this aspect of the project. What if we switched this around? Would that make us more productive?" Positioning it as a question allows everyone else to get on board and your creative ideas to be out there safely to be debated.

Real-Life "Betty"

"I've always worked in the information technology industry, which would seem rather rote and noncreative, but I've made it a goal of mine to really push the envelope and think outside the box in regard to my work. In one of my past jobs, I was completely invaluable to my boss because I was constantly doing research and bringing new ideas to her. I completely overhauled the networking system we had in place, which isn't something I was initially asked to do. But I proposed a system that would work better and more efficiently, effectively saving the company lots of money on operating and maintenance. Just because I'm not working in the creative industry doesn't mean that I can't be creative about problem solving."

—Tyler, 25, Kansas City

• • • • • •

To-Do List

* **Constantly be creative**. Approach creativity in terms of problem solving. How can you improve whatever you're working on?

* **Examine your work with a critical eye**. It doesn't sound like a creative process, but that's exactly what critiquing is.

* **Read!** The best ideas tend to come from synthesizing lots of information that you've absorbed from a variety of sources.

* **Know your mission backwards and forwards**. When you do, you'll better understand how creativity fits into your job.

* **Always have an idea handy**. Especially when you're going into a meeting, or just about any time. It can't hurt to have a creative take on how a project or proposal could be improved.

* **Offer solutions**. Not problems! Be creative by going to your boss with ideas about how to fix the speed bumps, rather than presenting the troubles.

Find a Niche

"I'm gonna go in early. I'm gonna get on a hardcore Erica Hahn cardio, and I'm gonna kick ass at it. And when I kick ass at cardio, it's gonna piss Christina off, but it won't matter because I'll be a kick-ass cardio God."

—Izzie Stevens, convincing herself it's a good idea to go after a cardio surgery specialty with Dr. Erica Hahn, even though it'll make her friend Christina Yang upset, on Grey's Anatomy

More often than not, the advice to "find a niche" in your industry is met with responses such as, "Well, I'm already an accountant!" Or, "I'm in the technology field. Isn't that specialty enough?" These days, it's not. Just look at the doctors from *Grey's Anatomy* again: To become truly great doctors, they all have chosen a specialty within surgery, whether it's focusing on the brain or cardiothoracic. They're all working toward an expertise. In the *Grey's* case above, Christina was always the cardio expert—a niche she solely owned among her peers and made her invaluable—until Izzie waltzed in with her own sudden interest in the area. The battle among these two to be the cardio specialist just underscores the importance of having an area that you own. Specializing gives you an edge, and while the *Grey's* doctors are required to do this, any career expert would tell you this strategy is essential for all professionals.

In the case of your career, finding a specialty could manifest itself in any number of ways, from specializing in a specific kind of law or developing an interest in tax accounting over small business accounting. Even in my field, I've chosen to specialize in entertainment writing and reporting, as opposed to dozens of other niches such as health, men's issues, or politics. If you want to really become valuable to your employer, become an expert in at least one area.

Examine Your Options

You may have garnered some special skills in college, but even that might not be specific enough in your field. Before you can target a specialty within your field, you've got to do your research. Use this step-by-step process to start figuring out your options:

1. **Don't rush it**. Employers won't expect you to waltz in to the office knowing exactly what your specialty should be. Most of the time, entry-level positions are designed to expose you to several different areas of the company so you can get a feel for what fits you best. It's important to remember that developing an expertise

takes time. At this point, it's just smart to have a loose idea of where you'd like your career to head.

2. **Take a look around**. After you get settled at work, check out the people who are a level above you to see where their strengths lie. It's likely that they have a specialty that helped them get promoted. If you're a young stockbroker, does it make sense to really know a certain area of trading, such as technology stocks or bonds? Do all of the publicists in your office who've been promoted from assistant have an area they specialize in, such as personal publicity or events? This'll give you an idea of what kinds of expertise are valuable to your company and industry and steer you in the right direction.

3. **Have a chat with your boss**. Ask your boss to lunch or a coffee break to talk about your options. What kind of specialists does the company especially need right now? Is the guy who's an expert on this specific kind of tax law about to move on to a different job? Would it be wise for you to possibly fill his shoes?

4. **Explore other departments**. See if you can't set up some meetings with colleagues or managers in other parts of the company. Usually people are open to these kinds of things, especially when you're young, new, and trying to figure out your future. At the meeting, pick the person's brain.

5. **Find a mentor**. After you've explored your options, target a person who has a job that you'd like and ask them to

be your mentor. You even may be able to shadow them for an afternoon. The relationship doesn't have to be anything formal. Just start by telling them you're interested in the special skill set that they have and ask if they wouldn't mind having lunch with you once a month to discuss your progress toward acquiring some of those skills.

Choose an Expertise

Briana, a 24-year-old chemist in Kansas City who spends her days doing research, chose to make her area of expertise organic synthesis chemistry. Come again? To anyone outside of the chemistry world, that sounds pretty foreign, but according to her, it's essential that she chose the area. "My job is based on research," she says. "And you can't really do research without having a specific area. You might not realize it, but chemistry is a huge subject. At my post-graduate level, it's obviously much more than what you might have learned in the tenth grade, which is the understanding the normal person has of the subject. So just like any career, we break it down into areas of expertise, including analytical, physical, and so on. I'm much more valuable having specific knowledge of one area rather than shallow, general knowledge of chemistry as a whole."

Career expert Brad Karsh says the need for expertise in a specific area of your field is more than just a necessity. "Companies don't want jacks-of-all-trades and masters of none," he says. "Maybe small companies where there are only a few people and everyone has to do everything, but in general, people want you to be an expert at something." Spherion's Chad Macy takes that one step further, explaining another benefit of being sharp in one particular area: "People will value your opinions more readily when they believe you know what you're talking about. You have the ability to be more strategic and really to start to be able to uncover those ideas because you understand what you're talking about."

On the Job
· · · · ·

Scenario: You've been in your entry-level marketing job for about nine months, which means you've only got about nine months left before you'll likely be promoted. Marketing on the Internet is huge, and your company seems to be headed in that direction. How do you fit into that picture, seeing as how you don't have any Internet marketing experience?

*

Quick Fix: Talk to your boss about getting put on a project that focuses on Internet marketing. See if you like it. If you do, it's worth thinking about making that your expertise. Of course, you already know marketing, but there is a special skill set for Internet marketing that you'll need to learn. At your company, this seems like a very shrewd move toward being promoted quickly.

Real-Life "Betty"

"I always knew that my path would lead me to the world of journalism. Once I got to college and started really getting into my magazine journalism major, I explored lots of different areas, including writing, editing, and design. Even the internships I had crossed over into all areas, allowing me to really try out lots of different areas of the business. But I quickly realized that being able to straddle everything wouldn't help me become an invaluable employee. And, honestly, would anyone hire me if I was a generalist? I mean, who wants someone who's good at everything but not great at anything? So I invested in graphic design, taking a few extra classes, and really targeted it as the part of journalism that I wanted to pursue. And now? I'm more valuable than ever to my employer because I'm totally an expert graphic designer."

—Kelsey, 25, New York City

• • • • • •

To-Do List

* **Find a mentor**. Know someone that has a skill set you're interested in acquiring? Ask them to be your mentor. Go to lunch every so often for advice and updates.

* **Check in with your boss**. Ask what kind of specialty and expertise your company or industry may be needing soon. Next, decide if that's something you're interested in pursuing.

* **Give yourself some time**. You don't have to have a specialty the moment you start a job. Take some time to consider lots of options.

* **Look around**. Lots of options will likely be right in front of you at work. What special functions do certain employees have? Can you develop a niche that'll make you invaluable? What kinds of skills are needed the most?

Become Tech Savvy

"He wants this company to be all about emails and IMs. But he's forgetting the original IM: notes attached to fruit baskets."

—Michael Scott, dogging on employee Ryan Howard, who quickly eclipsed him in terms of power at Dunder Mifflin because of his tech-savvy attitude, on The Office

In these plugged-in times, every good business runs on technology. Now that doesn't mean that the company has to literally be programming software or running a website, but all professionals today are going to be faced with technology every minute of the day, whether that means they're emailing clients, setting up Internet-based presentations, or teleconferencing into a meeting.

When we met the bunch over at Dunder Mifflin on *The Office*, they were never very tech savvy. The sales staff, Dwight and Jim, did most of their work via phone and the company certainly didn't have a website. But enter former temp employee and young professional Ryan, who quickly rose to corporate manager. While his antics are certainly amped up for comedy on the show, he showed fortitude by launching Dunder Mifflin Infinity, a website division that took the company into the future. While former boss Michael Scott refuses to see the value in Ryan's tech smarts, the corporate bigwigs did and quickly promoted him over his old boss.

The idea with technology as you enter the workforce isn't to start websites and launch tech programs, but you can imitate Ryan's tech-embracing nature. Being an employee who knows the ins and outs of technology will make you that much more valuable—and irreplaceable—to your company.

The Tech Savvier, the Better

No earlier generation has come into the workforce with such a great understanding of technology. In fact, you're likely one of the first people in your office who've never known a world without personal computers everywhere. Without a doubt, you should use this to your advantage.

Having a great working knowledge of programs and technology is one way to set yourself apart from the pack—especially from people who are older than you. At one point, *Ugly Betty's* Marc uses a viral video to improve his boss Wilhelmina's image. Granted, it's not exactly a professional pursuit, but Wilhelmina certainly needed his help to do it. "Every job is using more and more computer applications, systems, hardware, software. If you don't get on those bandwagons and start to become an expert at them, then you will be left behind," says

Spherion's Chad Macy. "As a young professional, if you spend the time building a foundation, you'll be good. Like, how does database structure work? How does Excel work?"

Start with this question: What kind of technology does your job use? Embrace whatever it is fully, even if that means taking an additional course or asking the IT department to give you a refresher course on the applications. "I would recommend that you really just soak up as much as you can," advises Macy. "One of the things I did was go through the Excel bible. If you have to, go to a training class, because when you go beyond just using something to understanding it, you become dangerous." Especially when you're young, it's easy to pick up technology. Simply put, that's why the older folks in your office struggle with it. "I always tell my teams, 'If you're not in love with our systems, then you don't understand them.' Once you understand the power of the technology your office has, you should be amazed."

Use Your Tech Savvy to Your Advantage

Many times, being a tech expert can give you access to the top brass and privileged information in your department or at your company. Career expert Brad Karsh offers up this personal example from when he was an entry-level employee: "When I first started working, I worked at an ad agency in Chicago. We had just moved to a new building. We had all these conference rooms with complicated audio-visual equipment. The senior executives, of course, didn't want to figure it out.

"I wasn't particularly good at it, but I figured out how to use it. Well, you know, at ad agencies, we're always showing tapes, right? We're always showing commercials. Guess who got invited to every meeting? Me—because I was literally the only guy who could work the equipment. Now, I didn't want to be typecast as the audio-visual boy, but the fact of the matter is that I was sitting in on a whole bunch of important meetings. I had access that no one else had, and it really gave me a leg up."

Older generations, especially, may see you as a whiz kid and an expert—much like *The Office*'s Ryan Howard—just from your basic knowledge. Perception is everything, so work that to your advantage. "If you become an expert at that, what happens is that people start coming to you as the expert," Macy says of other benefits to embracing technology. "In my own personal space, even though this isn't part of my job, my company sends me to different offices to train other managers or train other offices on our systems because they don't know it. People in my office will always come to me as the expert for that because they don't know it better than I do. I've prided myself in really learning my systems, learning the technology really well so I can get my job done faster. What takes people in Excel hours, I can do in seconds."

But Remember: Technology Is a Tool, Not a Strategy

Although you may want to rely solely on your tech knowledge, resist the urge. Just because you may use the technology on a daily basis, doesn't mean you're an expert on how it affects your business. As Karsh says, "One of the things I've seen new hires do is rely exclusively on technology. Recognize often that technology is a tool, not a strategy."

Don't let your savvy make you too big for your britches and manage your expectations of how far your skills really can take you. "I've seen students come in to a marketing job and say, 'Well, I don't even understand why I'm even reporting to all these 40-year-olds. I know MySpace. I know Facebook. I know YouTube better than they do. Shouldn't I be the one that's running the show?'" Karsh says. "Well, technology is a tool. Just because you can put the Excel spreadsheet in there faster, that's good and that's helpful, but I'm afraid a lot of new hires rely on that. That'd be like me walking in and saying, 'Well, I can type 80 words a minute, shouldn't I be the CEO?' Well, no. Sure, it'll help you work faster, but that doesn't necessarily mean that you're going to be the key guy because of that."

On the Job
• • • • •

Scenario: You've always thought of yourself as rather skilled when it comes to technology. But after just a few months on the job, it's clear you can't work many of the programs you need to perform your daily tasks. It's not like you're awful, but you realize you could be sharper. What's the best course of action?

✳

Quick Fix: Take a class on your own time! Or, better yet, see if your company will foot the bill for you to be upgraded. It's likely they'll want to invest in your technology skills.

Real-Life "Betty"

"Internet advertising has picked up a billionfold in the past few years. Because of this, a lot of new jobs in my industry have been added and have gone to significantly younger people. Positions that in television would have gone to people with 10 to 12 years of experience are suddenly going to 26-year-olds because they know and understand the product. Any new technology gives way for younger people to break in if they are willing to risk it and learn about it, and they're able to break in at much higher levels than before. On the other end of that,

I used to work with a girl who was one of our assistants. At 29 years old, she was much older than most at her level and, unfortunately for her, had been an assistant for six years. She couldn't work her computer, use her email, work our systems, use any Microsoft properties, and had a bad attitude that kept her from being promoted. Needless to say, the lack of technology skills—and her unwillingness to learn them—hindered her career greatly. If I learned anything from her, it was to know my computer backwards and forwards!"

—Elizabeth, 26, New York City

• • • • • •

To-Do List

* **Always sharpen your technology skills**. Keeping up to date with the latest and greatest in technology will make you irreplaceable at the office.

* **Offer to help others**. Showing your tech smarts adds to your credibility and whiz-kid nature.

* **Realize the limitations of technology**. It's not a replacement for strategy or understanding your industry.

Gather, Devour, and Respond to Feedback

"Last year, my performance review started with Michael asking me what my hopes and dreams were, and it ended with him telling me he could bench-press 190 pounds, so I don't really know what to expect."

—*Receptionist Pam Beesly, about her meandering performance assessment, on* The Office

Today, the workplace is a frenzy of assessments—project post-mortems, self-appraisals, and performance reviews—not to mention all kinds of gratuitous ratings and rankings. The list goes on and on. Even though some of these assessments may seem rather rote and uninspired—like the standard but decidedly wacky reviews, which Pam Beesly references above, administered by uber-doofus boss Michael Scott on *The Office*—they are all important to your continued success. Good employees take cues and feedback in whatever form it comes every day. And the best employees? They constantly assess themselves and their work to see how they can improve.

If the crew from *The Office* actually does perform some sort of regular self-assessment to improve their productivity and grow professionally, the viewers certainly don't see it. Dunder Mifflin might just be the least self-aware work environment ever. But that doesn't mean you can't be personally responsive: A superior will undoubtedly scrutinize every task you perform, and every task you perform should be scrutinized by you too.

Seek Feedback

In today's corporate environment, performance reviews are a yearly occurrence typically loathed by all parties involved because of their sterilized nature. To avoid being blindsided in those types of assessment situations, however, it's smart to look for cues as to how you're doing on a day-to-day basis. Without a doubt, you'll receive all kinds of assessment and feedback in your job: everything from off-the-cuff suggestions and notes from a coworker to what you may overhear being said about your work ethic in the bathroom. The key is to recognize when you're being given suggestions for improvement, and then to take action.

You can bet that your boss will value you more if you're constantly improving and working toward goals rather than picking up the pieces after a particularly hard performance review once a year. How do you go about constantly seeking feedback? Here are some of the easiest ways:

Talk to your boss. Think of Betty and Daniel or Marc and his diva-boss Wilhelmina on *Ugly Betty*. Both employee-boss relationships are defined by an honest back-and-forth about expectations. Like these two young professionals, the No. 1 way to know how you're doing is to casually ask your boss or other superior. It doesn't necessarily have to be in any kind of traditional, scary sit-down situation. Just be like *30 Rock*'s Liz Lemon, who regularly checks in with her boss Jack Donaghy if she needs to talk.

"Many companies don't have a sophisticated human resources organization that says every February we do an appraisal of our employees," says John McKee, a career and life success coach based in Los Angeles. He advises: "Request that 90 days after you're hired, you have the chance to sit with your boss and have a 'How's it going?' conversation. If you have concerns or recommendations, it's good to disclose those to your boss at the time. You have to figure out how to have an ongoing stream of communication that isn't seen as being irritating, but instead seen as adding value. Another easy way to do that is by suggesting a weekly update of what you're working on and what you plan to accomplish. Bosses usually love this. It keeps you front and center and makes you more accessible."

Career counselor Dan King adds: "The best sort of conversations with your boss are on sort of an impromptu basis: 'Here's what I've been thinking. Does that make sense to you?' Having that sort of discussion."

The benefit of asking for regular feedback from your boss? Hallie Crawford, a career coach and founder of

Authentically Speaking in Georgia, says, "It's going to show that you're proactive and care about your job. If you want more feedback, if you want to be more proactive, speak up and just ask for it."

Keep your ears open around the office. McKee suggests literally wandering around your workplace and chatting with coworkers. "It's those informal conversations that can really help someone to get a true handle on what's going on," he advises, "instead of those formal assessment projects."

Bounce concerns off colleagues. Coworkers are another great resource for informal feedback. Granted, they're also looking for assessment of their own work, but they can give you tips about what you might be doing right or wrong on the job, especially if they're more senior or experienced than you.

Pay close attention at meetings. You likely won't be publicly scrutinized, but you can pick up on what's going well—and what's not—just by listening in a group session. Conversation about projects or tasks around the office will undoubtedly turn to what's working and what's not. If projects you're responsible for come up, take notes about what's said and fix the problems before they get worse.

Feel out clients and customers. This informal process involves casually chatting with those people outside your company whom you interact with on a regular basis. Are they happy with the level of customer service you're giving them? How are they reacting to your work? What could you do better? Figure out what the sticking points are and address them before they get back to your superiors.

Consult your mentor. Follow the lead of *Damages'* young lawyer Ellen Parsons, who often seeks feedback from Tom Shayes, a seasoned lawyer at her firm. If you want direct feedback on how you're doing, schedule a time to talk to your unbiased mentor, who'll undoubtedly give you sage advice from a personal perspective.

Be Your No. 1 Critic

Despite all the best feedback in the world from outside sources, it's unlikely that anyone knows you better than you do. That is, as long as you're being honest with yourself about your performance. So you be the judge: How are you doing? What areas do you need to improve? How can you better play to your strengths?

When I suggest you be your No. 1 critic, I simply mean that you should dissect all your assignments or projects at work after they're over to see how you could have done better. For instance, much of my job at *Entertainment Weekly* consists of me writing and reporting, naturally, entertainment news. After I turn in a story, I watch carefully as it goes up the chain of editors. What things are they correcting? How did they reword a particularly tricky paragraph so it was clear to readers? What reporting was the story missing? Where am I a repeat offender?

Honestly, my busy editors rarely have time to sit down with me after each assignment to discuss the details of what was right and wrong. I'm lucky if I get an email acknowledging that I turned in my copy! And what's the point anyway? I usually can tell where the problem areas are by closely monitoring my work. The most important part of this process is to be honest with yourself: You know when you've screwed up and when you've done well. If it's the former, don't dwell on it longer than it takes for you to learn your lesson. Commit the right way to handle the task to memory, vow not to make the same mistake again, and move on.

On the Job
• • • • •

Scenario: It's three months into your job and your boss wants to have an informal chat to discuss how you've been progressing so far. He tells you that you needn't prepare anything and to just come ready to chat. How does a smart employee such as yourself approach the situation?

✳

Quick Fix: Prepare something, of course, but don't make it so obvious! Think through what your conversation will likely cover and what points you definitely want to make. Try writing down every major task you've completed and the reasons why each one either did or didn't go well. You'll show your boss you've been both performing and thinking about how to increase your productivity.

Real-Life "Betty"

"I've been working in my ad sales job for a year and four months and have had one formal review from my bosses. In my experience, I was pretty confident going in that they would have mostly positive things to say, and certainly everything they said was helpful to hear. Because I have three bosses, the work flow is constant and overwhelming at times. I often find myself focusing so intently on their requests, needs, and direction that I lose sight of monitoring myself in the whole process. Is it valuable to hear how someone else views my work flow? Of course. Is it helpful for them to bring up a point or habit that I too often overlook? Definitely. Are they right? For the most part, yes. But I've learned that through checking on myself from time to time is the best way for me to catch problems before they get out of hand."

—Lauren, 23, New York City

• • • • • •

To-Do List

* **Constantly assess yourself**. Formal, but typically infrequent, feedback from bosses is standard, but look to yourself first to identify areas of improvement. You'll be seen as a proactive employee.

* **Use every opportunity as a chance to learn and grow**. Plain and simple, learn from your mistakes.

* **Clue in your boss about how you're improving**. Avoid awkward queries by coming up with the ways you can improve at work.

* **React positively to assessment from your boss**. An employee who's willing to change is infinitely more valuable.

* **Mask your requests for feedback**. A casual conversation about work is the perfect time to slip in covert, but essential, questions about how you're progressing.

* **Turn feedback into goals**. When your boss or a co-worker makes a suggestion of how to improve your work, turn it into a goal you can work toward.

Part Four

Go Beyond Office Hours

Diversify Your Personal Life

"Hey, Rhoda, would you do me a favor? Please don't start treating me like I'm in show business. I mean, I'm still working in the newsroom, huh? This is just something I'm doing for fun, OK?"

—*Mary Richards, telling her best friend Rhoda about the new play she's been cast in, on* The Mary Tyler Moore Show

All work and no play makes Mary a dull girl. That adage couldn't be truer when it comes to *your* career too. I've been plugging away for 15 chapters telling you to focus on your image, build relationships, and work your buns off in the professional realm, but now it's time to focus on your personal life. Take a cue from Mary Richards and have out-of-office interests that will help you blow off steam while also propelling you forward professionally. With the caveat that she's a character from a TV show in a make-believe world, Mary Richards is still a great example of being a well-rounded young professional. While she works hard—often staying well past the evening newscast and doting on her boss, Lou Grant—she plays hard too. As the quote above shows personal pursuits, she's clearly got diverse interests.

Mary's extracurriculars help to make her a better employee, especially in her position as a news producer. Her role in that play could spark an idea for a great story on the news, or simply allow her to get her mind off her busy day at work. Employees who are happier at home are happier at work. The same goes for you too. Stressed out at work? Get a hobby, spend time with friends, and enjoy nonwork activities; it'll do you good professionally.

Find Something to Love Besides Your Job

Remember that time before you were career-obsessed? What'd you do for fun? How'd you blow off steam? It'd do you some good to rediscover a personal passion. Even if it's somewhat job related—say you're a nurse who volunteers at a free clinic—make sure it's time well spent that is a release from daily work pressures. Or, your outside activity could be a healthy diversion from your career, such as joining a knitting circle, book club, rugby team, or other social group. *Ugly Betty*'s Marc, for instance, spends his free time with a personal interest: catching up on old movies. Alternately, *How I Met Your Mother*'s womanizer Barney blows off steam by playing lazer tag.

Career coach Hallie Crawford speaks to the idea of a person's passion benefiting their workplace demeanor. "Even if your career is the most fulfilling thing in your life, you still don't want to put all your eggs in one basket," she says, making the case for a wide variety of interests. "There actually have been studies about this, but people who have lives outside of work and have better work-life balance are happier, more productive employees."

That happiness and fulfillment affects your career in so many ways. "You can even go to the extreme of saying that professionals who are happy personally get sick less, they experience less stress, and therefore, they're going to be at their jobs more. There's the mental aspect of it, where you're going to be more efficient and happier," Crawford says. "You'll think more creatively and problem solve better. Then there are the physical ramifications of it. If you don't have any sort of personal life, you'll experience greater stress, which will affect your performance at work. They say an artist will work on a painting for a while and then need to take a break to get an inspired thought about it. The same idea goes for anybody."

Embrace Nonindustry Friends

Due to the small and somewhat incestuous media world that I work in, I tend to have friends who have very similar jobs. We sit around at bars and rehash who's moving and shaking in media and dissect our workplace glories and gripes. But that gets old so quickly; I *so* cherish those friends of mine who couldn't tell you who was last on the cover of *Vanity Fair*. While talking shop is always a good time, talking anything *but* shop is often just what the career doctor ordered. I can't tell you how many times I've met up with my other magazine buddies for happy hour and immediately put the kibosh on industry talk. It's exhausting if your personal life is filled only with work-related topics.

The wisdom here is to spend time procuring friends who are outside your career bubble. If you're an accountant, find a friend who's an actor. You're a scientist? Befriend someone in finance. The five friends on *How I Met Your Mother*—Barney, Ted, Marshall, Lily, and Robin—are exemplary: They all work in different industries, and, thus, their friendships extend beyond just work gripes. The easiest way to do this, obviously, is to meet your friends' friends and steal them—what I affectionately call "friend poaching." Meet them at a party and invite them for a cocktail the next week; it's likely they're looking to connect with someone to befriend outside their industry too.

On the Job
• • • • •

Scenario: You're loving your job as a publicist and you've recently joined the Public Relations Society of America, a national professional group for professionals in publicity. You also volunteer by doing pro bono publicity for a non-profit. Because you're passionate about your field, signing up for all of these work-related extracurriculars seemed like a good idea at the time. But now, your work is suffering because you're sick of what amounts to overdosing on publicity. What's the best way to fix this problem?

✳

Quick Fix: Lose at least one of the outside publicity obligations and choose an activity that's totally different but that you're also passionate about. How about volunteering to read to underprivileged kids? Joining a volleyball team? Learning to scuba dive? A random after-work activity will propel you to focus your publicity smarts at work, rather than funnel all your great ideas into unpaid positions that only serve to drain you.

Real-Life "Betty"

"How important is it for me to have an outlet or hobby or passion outside of work? Simply put, it's essential. I'm a graphic designer, and through both my full-time and freelance careers, I've made it a point to always do the things I love. In fact, that's why I went freelance. Whether it's knitting with friends at a café or walking in the park or, for the most part, traveling, having distance from the grind of the office helps me have a better outlook at work. Traveling, in particular, has given me a new sense of independence and a little bit more confidence, and that wonderfully creeps into my professional life as well. The best advice I ever received was from an alum of my college who said, 'Always know why you're at your job. Whether it's the money, the people, a great mentor, the fulfillment, whatever. You should always have a reason why you're there.' For me, this couldn't be truer. I do my job so I can live the life I want outside of the office. It's always better if you work to live, rather than live to work."

—Särah, 28, New York City

• • • • • •

To-Do List

* **Have a hobby or two**. Out-of-the-office passions make your in-office attitude sunnier.

* **Build a diverse group of friends**. Don't limit yourself to friends who are in your industry. You'll more quickly get sick of your job that way.

* **Rediscover a passion**. Spend your nonworking time developing an interest that you may have ignored, or never knew you had in the first place!

* **Find a happy place**. Work may not always be so pleasant, but what you do with your free time should make you smile.

LESSON 17

Strike a Healthy Work-Life Balance

"Do you realize that this is the first time since mom died that we haven't all been together on his birthday? It's fine, Betty. I just hope it's all worth it."

—Hilda Suarez, berating her sister Betty for missing their dad's birthday party for a late night at work, on Ugly Betty

Ugly Betty's Betty Suarez often struggles with how to be an on-the-ball employee yet remain dedicated to her biggest out-of-office diversion, her family. Like the example above shows, Betty often lost the battle to work, especially at the beginning, as she found herself logging long hours and missing her dad's birthday celebration. An unlikely situation for you, hopefully, but it brings up the all-important issue of maintaining a proper work-life balance. Even though you may be tempted to put your personal life on hold when your professional life rumbles to a start, you can't do that forever.

Like Betty, your personal life—whether that means your dedication to your family, a significant other, and whatever other personal obligations you have—shouldn't go by the wayside just because you're working. When you're new to the job, however, it will no doubt be difficult to come to a happy medium between the two. Even though you may feel like your work should take priority, remember that you're entitled to have a life too, and your happiness in that realm has a direct effect on your productivity. Just like your boss and coworkers, you've got a personal life that needs tending.

A Managed Personal Life Means a Managed Professional Life

When you think about work-life balance, it's easy to equate it to work-fun balance. But, for all intents and purposes, what it means is striking a healthy balance between what you need to do to get ahead professionally with what you need to do to stay sane and tend to your personal life.

"There are a lot of people who think work-life balance means, 'I feel like I'm not having enough fun because I'm working all the time, so I need to figure out how to get more fun in,'" says Sara K. Collins, a career consultant in Washington, D.C. "That's important, but work-life balance includes the little things, like when you're going to get the car in for inspection. If you wait until it breaks down, then you're really going to have big problems."

Consider all of those other life-maintenance items that you need to work into your schedule. A huge component is smart time management. "I remember when I was in graduate school there was a time-management guru who came and talked to us," Collins says. "He broke down the week, hour by hour, for us. He said that if you spend one hour for each of your three meals, which seemed like a lot, then that subtracts this many hours from your week. He just went through the whole week. Then, he said you still had this certain number of free hours to do whatever you want. I thought I was really doing something wrong because I didn't have that many hours!

"It wasn't until later, of course, after the question-and-answer session was over, that I realized he assumed you have a cook and maid and a personal assistant and you didn't need to network, job search, and have downtime. But you still need to do all of that. You still need to go to the bank. If you hear somebody tell you that there's some magic formula for how you can be super-efficient and work your ass off at your job and be super-successful and have a ton of extracurriculars and maintain strong relationships and your health, you just can't. You can't have it all at the same time." To boot, a good use of personal time is to simply take a breather and decompress from work.

It's easy to come out of college thinking you can take on the world—and I've been preaching that in this book, for sure—but before world domination comes things such as dentists. "You move to a new city, and your childhood dentist isn't sending you a six-month reminder anymore," says Collins, who advises that figuring out these little things in your personal life will keep you de-stressed. "Just things like, 'OK, well we want cable in our new apartment. Who's going to spend the four hours waiting for the guy to show up?' Right after college, I'd joke around that I was a baby grownup. While I felt like I had graduated from childhood, I suddenly still felt very naive—not in the traditional sense—because there was a whole bunch of things that I never thought about."

Know What You're Getting Into

To achieve a work-life balance that suits your tastes, the first step is to pick an industry or line of work that's conducive to what you're expecting. Look at the crew from *Friends:* Joey was an actor, which afforded him a lifestyle with loads of free time. For comparison sake, Chandler had a corporate job that required more out of him. At one point he even had to commute from New York City to his company's office in Oklahoma, which wasn't so great for his personal life or relationship with Monica. "Everybody has different ideas about what balance is anyway," says Collins. "But if you want to be CEO of GM someday, or if you want to be a surgeon, you are going to have to make some big sacrifices."

If that's not how you want to spend your twenties, don't head down that career trail. "If that totally goes against your vision of what your life is going to be, you may need to pick a different way. The best thing you can do there is just network with people and find out what lies ahead so that you're not surprised. You don't want to wake up and say, 'I'm 37 and I don't have a social life. What happened?'"

Combating waking up with such a revelation may be as easy as setting some boundaries. "Don't respond to BlackBerry messages on a date," advises Collins with a laugh. That would seem like a given to most people, but your boss may expect you to be on call all the time. So, the thing to do is be clear and up-front with your boss from the get-go. Establish what is expected of you from day one and make sure your priorities jive with your boss's needs. "You need to set some boundaries, especially if your boss is overzealous or the company's culture is to be on call 24/7," Collins adds. "Alternatively, you may need to think about whether that is the right place for you."

Learn to Say "No"

This is a lesson I've been learning the hard way, and I still haven't fully processed it. I've never been a person to turn down any opportunity, personally or professionally, but the busier I get in both realms, the more and more I realize that "no" is a word I have to employ. "Sorry, no, I can't stay out for that drink because I have to get up in the morning." "No, I shouldn't take on these extra responsibilities with the networking organization I work for on the side." These are responses I'm practicing, and you should too.

I've often found myself in hot water by over-scheduling my time. Work-related events or parties overlap with time that I was supposed to be working with an extracurricular organization or meeting up with friends and family. Or, even worse, those times I've had to cancel life-maintenance appointments such as meeting with my financial planner, the dentist, or even my hairdresser. Of course, just like me, you want it all, but that's nearly impossible. Says Collins: "The work hard, play hard life is not sustainable."

On the Job
· · · · ·

Scenario: To your endless frustration, you're often logging 65 to 70 hours a week, resulting in a personal life that's in shambles. Your boss keeps you on call nearly 24/7 and doesn't think anything of it, but this isn't what you thought you signed up for. How do you approach a possible change?

✳

Quick Fix: Talk with your boss, who's hopefully open to the discussion, about possibly setting some boundaries and reducing your workload. Your boss may not realize how much you're doing. However, this quandary is like walking a tightrope: You signed up for the position. It may just be a case of putting in your dues for a year or two and managing your personal life better until your job becomes less demanding.

Real-Life "Betty"

"My job is ideal for the work-life balance that I wanted. I'm a pharmacist, and I chose this career partly because I knew it'd allow me to balance my professional life with my personal life. My family has been, and always will be, super important to me, and I'm intent on having my own family very soon. The hours are, for the most part, regular. I have friends in other industries who have crazy hours; they sit at their desks into the wee hours of the morning. I just knew that wasn't for me! When I leave the office, I check out for good and don't take my work home with me."

—*Katie, 25, Waterloo, Iowa*

• • • • • •

To-Do List

* **Set aside time for personal tasks**. A tidy personal life means a less-stressful, and more productive, professional life.

* **Know what you're getting into**. If you can't handle the heavy demands of a certain job, it may be worth looking into other fields or industries.

* **Just say no**. Whether in your personal or professional life, there are times you'll have to bow out to

keep your sanity. It's unrealistic to think you can do everything.

* **Look to your support system for help**. Whether that's relying on the family members who are nearby or procuring a de facto family of friends, build a network that can help you when personal problems arise.

* **Leave work at work**. It's easier said than done, but keeping your spheres as separate as possible is always advisable.

Keep Up Your Guard

"I want people to cut loose. I want people making out in closets. I want people hanging from the ceiling, lampshades on their heads. I want this to be a Playboy mansion party."

—*Michael Scott, inappropriately hoping his employees will go out of control at the office holiday party, on* The Office

The demands of today's workplace stretch beyond clock-out time and into your personal time. But even when you're not technically on the clock, your professionalism must remain intact. After-work happy hours, weekend-long company retreats, business trips, off-site projects, and holiday parties are undoubtedly less structured than regular work, but they're still extensions of your job and require the same controlled behaviors you'd normally muster in the office. They're not occasions for you to pull out your keg-party persona.

Most of the time, these beyond-the-office events will be fun. Just look to the holiday parties that have been thrown by the Dunder Mifflin crew on *The Office*, the photo shoots on *Ugly Betty*, or the after-hours socializing that goes on at the bar across the street from Seattle Grace on *Grey's Anatomy*. In these situations, however, the young professionals often mistakenly let loose a little too much—losing their professional wits, while taking the fun too far into ridiculous antics and ill-advised hookups. Even though you're technically out of the office, you've got to bring an on-the-clock mentality to these types of outings. Michael Scott's sentiments spell out exactly the kind of behavior you don't want to exhibit. Heed his words as a warning, and take the following words as good advice.

You're Always Representing Your Company

"The most important thing to remember is that you are on 24/7," says Colleen Rickenbacker, etiquette expert and author of *Be on Your Best Business Behavior.* "I don't care if you're on a picnic someplace. If someone sees you and says, 'Oh, where do you work?' They will associate your actions, whatever they may be, with your company. How you work, how you act, it all comes back in a full circle."

Sure, it may have been a hard day, or maybe even a hard year by the time the end-of-year office holiday party rolls around. But think about it: Is a work function really the place to make a fool of yourself? "Don't let the setting fool you," advises Rickenbacker. "Just because you're at a bar, you're at a restaurant, you're at somebody's party, it doesn't matter," she adds. "You never come out of your professional mode. People relate the personal you to the professional you. You might be thinking, Well, what makes the difference? These are all twentysomethings or thirtysomethings. Well, people grow up, people tell other people, and people do other things. It all comes around."

Just as the first five chapters of this book spelled out, your image is on display, and even though you're not in the office, it will be scrutinized. As is nearly always the case, actions speak louder than words, and you don't want to be water-cooler fodder the next morning. "You can't be dancing on a table or drinking so much that you're under the table," Rickenbacker adds. "Also, you need to watch how you dress. You can't come out in this unbelievable, risqué, working-the-streets kind of outfit or some kind of loud outfit. You have to represent yourself well."

According to Rickenbacker, repercussions encompass more than just a hangover: "The people you're socializing with could end up having a hand in your career down the line. Who's to say you're not going to be looking for a job down the line, and someone asks them for a reference? Sadly enough, the older you get, the worse it gets. People see you, and they know you. You have to keep your image up, and it has to be a good image."

Heed These Golden Rules

Any off-site function can be a recipe for disaster if you kick back too much and lose yourself. Remember when *Ugly Betty's* Betty Suarez went to an after-hours networking event with fellow assistants Amanda and Marc and had one too many martinis? They all ended up blabbing parts of a big *Mode* secret, which put their jobs in jeopardy. Simply put, the best advice is to be responsible and stay in control in these situations. Here are a few pointers that'll keep you out of trouble:

Show your face. Skipping workplace social events without a good excuse is bad form. Others, and unfortunately especially the office gossips, will take note of who's missing. Not showing gives the impression that you don't want to socialize with fellow employees and that you might not be invested in your job. Take a chance and go. You just may surprise yourself by having a good time.

Lay off the booze. It's so tempting to keep drinking, especially when the cocktails are on the company or a client. Cavorting wildly with Santa Claus at the holiday party, like Christina McKinney did on *Ugly Betty*, may look like fun, but you'll regret your drunken missteps or face major repercussions if you make a fool of yourself in front of clients. "You must remember, you have to see these people tomorrow or on Monday or whenever it is you're going to see them again," says Rickenbacker. "At these functions, even though it might be a social gathering, who's to say the CEO isn't going to be there? Or the son, daughter, cousin, or assistant to the CEO? They're going to go home and say, I saw so-and-so, and he was just drunk and all over the place." All of this is not to say that you can't drink at all. Just know your limits and stay within them.

Keep topics light. No need to split hairs about religion or politics with coworkers or clients; just stick to smaller talk. It never hurts to have a few conversation starters in your back pocket either: subjects such as the weather, upcoming holidays and vacations, sports, and entertainment.

Remember your manners. Especially if you're off-site with clients, all the social graces, such as chewing with your mouth closed and eating with the right fork, are expected. If you're nervous about your actions, just take your cues from a put-together coworker or even one of the clients. Rickenbacker warns: "Sometimes, mistakes in terms of manners can be very costly because people don't forget the first impression."

Circulate. One major faux pas young professionals commit at out-of-the-office gatherings or while with clients is solely socializing within their department or core group of work friends. This is a chance to get out there and let people know who you are! See it as a networking opportunity—or just a chance to put faces with the names you've heard around the office.

Be gracious. Someone spent time planning the event: picking the space, the entertainment, and everything else right down to the napkins on the table. If the party isn't up to your standards, don't be vocal about it. You only have to grin and bear it for a couple of hours.

On the Job
• • • • •

Scenario: At your first after-hours work social event, you're three beers in but holding it together well when a coworker challenges you to a round of beer pong. The atmosphere is a tad rowdy, but no one else is playing drinking games and all of your bosses are close at hand. Do you accept his challenge?

✳

Quick Fix: Heck no! This kind of reckless behavior is just asking for it. Make a polite getaway.

Real-Life "Betty"

"There's always the cautionary tale about not drinking too much at office events. I think the most famous of these in my industry, which is ad buying, is the 'Party Pooper,' which made the Page Six gossip column in the *New York Post*. During the big ad-buying time in May a couple years ago, a brand-new, fresh out of college assistant buyer went to parties every night of the week, which is totally the norm. But, after the long week of presentations and parties, she let loose at the week's last party and had way too much to drink. She couldn't hold it, crapped in her pants in the middle of the party, and had to be carried out. She was subsequently fired, and had to switch industries. She's still talked about all the time."

—*Elizabeth, 26, New York City*

• • • • • •

To-Do List

* **Remember you're always representing your company**. Your best, professional behavior is required even during social functions.

* **Don't let your guard down**. Keep the line between personal and professional clear whenever you're

with work people, even if it's just a few of your closest work friends.

* **Watch your alcohol consumption**. Drinking too much is the easiest way to make a fool of yourself. Set a limit and stick to it.

* **Have manners**. My mom always told my siblings and me that we were to eat at the dinner table like Queen Elizabeth was sitting with us. You'd do well to heed this advice anytime you're hanging with work people or clients too.

* **Keep conversation light**. Small talk is best, especially with coworkers, bosses, or clients whom you don't know well.

* **Come off as interested**. Introduce yourself, circulate, ask questions, and listen.

Embrace Overtime Without Being a Pushover

"What Daniel is trying to say is kiss your loved ones good-bye. Expect to come home to dead pets!"

—Mode *creative director Wilhelmina Slater, reminding her staff that they're chained to their desks, on* Ugly Betty

Few and far between are the days at *Entertainment Weekly* when I leave at what is our supposed quitting time of 6 PM. In the scene above, Betty and the rest of the crew at *Mode* find themselves in a similar after-hours situation and seem to be working nearly round the clock, especially Amanda, Marc, and Betty, the youngest of the professionals in the office. If they're not plugging away, they're certainly on call to be whisked back into service at a moment's notice. It's not enviable to be expected to work a 50- or 60-hour workweek, but when you're young, many times it's just part of putting in your dues.

Remember when *Mode* was scrambling to come up with a new concept after their post-apocalyptic Christmas idea was snatched? Bosses Wilhelmina and Daniel told the crew to forget their social lives for a couple of days and spend some quality time at the office. Even if you're not on the crazy schedule of the media industry, don't expect immunity from overtime, especially when you're starting out. In fact, you should realize that more often than not, you'll be pulled in on these types of things simply because you're young and energetic. But this doesn't have to be such a bad thing. In fact, your boss will likely see you as an asset if you're willing to pitch in whenever, wherever. Don't fret, though, just rewards come to those who pull their weight.

Flexibility Is Your Friend

We've discussed going the extra mile and becoming irreplaceable. Embracing overtime is another aspect of those concepts. Your boss will undoubtedly find you that much more valuable if you're the employee who's willing to stay late. Come promotion time, if your boss is deciding between you, who clocked out at 4:59 every day, and the gal who worked a Saturday here and there and checked her work from home once in a while, who do you think will get that salary bump and new title?

The key is being flexible: Play every situation by ear to figure out if you may need to put in some extra time to make your part of it perfect. Honestly, there's no reason to put in overtime just for the sake of it, but when you need to, be prepared to do it with a smile.

When working on an especially time-consuming project, Ted Mosby, the architect on *How I Met Your Mother*, often found himself sneaking back into the office for late-night work sessions. Editor-in-chief Deborah Ohrn, at Meredith Corporation, can think of many times where her young employees, like Ted, pulled her out of a bind by pitching in beyond regular office hours. "These are the young people who have the skill that we really depend on," she says. "One pulled an all-nighter recently, which honestly is an anomaly, but we wouldn't have gotten the project done without that."

I'm certainly not advocating that you stay overnight at the office—at least not very often—but that sort of passion just may take you to the next level. "The enthusiasm is huge," adds Ohrn. "There are too many of us now who are a little bit burned out or you've just been doing it too long. To be around that fresh enthusiasm is just a joy—it's just a joy! Being hungry is a good thing!"

Strike a Balance

At this stage in your career, of course you'd think you should always be the one who stays late or is on call if an after-hours task crops up. But that's not exactly the case. Just like your boss, you have a social life that needs tending. And you shouldn't be the only one to suffer.

Unfortunately, younger employees, especially those without kids or ones who don't have to commute far, tend to get slammed more than other employees who are parents. The key here is to not be taken advantage of by your employer just because you're young. Honestly, though, it's a matter of expectations: What did your boss tell you about working more than seven or eight hours a day when you were hired? Is there a pecking order? Is it simply that you'll eventually graduate from being the night owl in the office and new underlings will take over? If things get out of control, it's worth requesting a chat with your boss about how responsibilities could possibly be redistributed or how you can get all your work done in a timely fashion going forward.

Reap the Benefits of Your Long Hours

Listen, it's rarely a joyful occasion to have to stay past closing time, but if you have to, why not make the best of the situation and see how you can benefit? First, there's a good chance you may get paid overtime for any hours you work past a normal workday. Granted, the taxman tends to eat up much more of your paycheck when you make more, but you won't mind staying late a few times a week when you get that direct deposit with the extra cash. If you don't know whether you get paid time and a half for additional hours, make sure to ask human resources, although it's best to ask such questions at the time of hiring. In some industries, such as media where Betty and I work, overtime pay is standard at big companies.

Second, check with others around your office, or consult whatever workplace guide you were given, about other benefits of staying late. Many workplaces spring for dinner after a certain hour and, at least in New York City where most office workers commute to work on mass transportation, your employer may even send you home in a taxi after a certain hour. Often, when I'm staying past 9 PM, I comfort myself with the thought of a tasty plate of Chinese food at my desk and a warm cab ride home.

Additionally, it never hurts to check on the official policy about comp time or possibly coming in late the next morning. Sometimes, to compensate for making employees stay late, companies may offer additional vacation days or a delayed morning after a long night.

On the Job

• • • • •

Scenario: Tonight is the birthday party you've been planning for your best friend for the past few weeks, but at about 5:30 PM, you get an email from your boss asking if you can stay late to finish up a quick project he needs for a midday meeting tomorrow. You're typically pleased to get the overtime hours, but for once, you really can't stay late. Do you skip the birthday party you planned or wiggle your way out of the work?

✳

Quick Fix: Neither! Explain your situation to your boss. No reasonable person is so unsympathetic that they'll make you miss a party that you planned. Ask if there might be someone else who can stay late this one time—and add that you'd be happy to fill in any other evening. Alternatively, offer to take the work home to finish after the party or to arrive early in the morning to finish up the project.

Real-Life "Betty"

"After a few months on the job, I felt pretty comfortable with my basic fact-checking responsibilities, so I started looking for ways to keep the job challenging and keep learning new things. My goal was to write, so I started sending story ideas to the editor in charge of the back of the book. She asked my boss if it was OK if I wrote items, and my boss said yes as long as my normal responsibilities didn't suffer.

"I started writing about one item a month. I never turned down an opportunity, even if it meant writing on my own time, at home, on the weekends. Now I'm writing three to four small items a month! I don't care if I have to stay late at the office or work at home in order to be able to do what I want. This is all keeping me busy and entertained at work, but in the big picture I'm also cultivating skills I'll need for a career in publishing-writing, working with editors, and pitching ideas."

—Bridget, 23, New York City

• • • • • •

To-Do List

* **Be flexible**. Realize that overtime is likely a part of your career at this early stage. Figure out a reasonable way to fit it into your life.

* **Jump on opportunities to pitch in where needed**. Bosses love a flexible employee—and who knows exactly how that late-night project may impact your career.

* **Realize the benefits of working late**. You possibly may get additional pay, meals in the evening, transportation home, and comp days. Check with your cohorts or human resources.

* **Don't become dependent on overtime**. For the most part, you should be able to complete your assigned tasks during the day. If you find yourself staying late every night, either you've got too much to do or you're not efficient during the day.

* **Make sure others know your efforts**. Deliberately send emails and copy your boss when you're there late into the evening; it'll make your superiors aware of your extra efforts.

* **Don't be a pushover**. Just because you may be the lowest on the totem pole doesn't mean you should be working 80-hour weeks.

LESSON 20

Keep Learning

"This class is phase one of my career: I write, I get published, I work my way to editor, and then I can run a magazine."

—*Betty Suarez, telling her family about the writing class she's taking during lunch, on* Ugly Betty

For *Ugly Betty's* Betty Suarez, reaching her goal of running her own magazine requires professional experience beyond that of her job as the assistant to the editor-in-chief of *Mode*. While she may have spent four years in college writing for the college paper, she found herself in a job that wasn't giving her the skills that she needed. Answering her boss's phone and tracking down electronic wheelchairs for him wasn't putting pencil to paper. It wasn't until her friend Gio, *Mode's* old sandwich guy, pointedly asked her what she had written recently that she realized she wasn't actually doing what she set out to when she originally scored the job at *Mode*. It was time for her to make a change and invest a little bit of her own time into keeping her career on track.

So what'd Betty do? Employing the mantra, "What you

can't get at work, get elsewhere," she enrolled in a writing class during her lunch hour. Like Betty, furthering your education in the professional realm is always a shrewd move if you're looking to evolve your career. Just look at what it did for Ryan, the former temp employee on *The Office*. He was working on his MBA, and before anyone knew it, he jumped to the corporate job of his dreams, vaulting past his dubious boss Michael Scott. You can do it too—just figure out what's right for you, explore your options, and make your move.

Determine the Right Move for You

Hopefully, you don't see yourself in your current position in five or ten years. To that end, the first step toward your continued education—and career advancement—is simple: Ask yourself how you want to develop professionally. Or, more precisely, what additional education or skills do you need to have the job you want? As a young professional, you likely already have at least a four-year degree, but the question is: How can you take that and build on it toward your career goal?

All too often young professionals who are discouraged with their current career track or those who are overly eager to keep their career moving and shaking make rash decisions about where to go, without consulting someone. You can learn from those who've made mistakes before you. "There are so many people in the past, at least, who didn't know what they wanted to do, and so they just went to law school," says career coach Hallie Crawford. "That's when you have to think harder about jumping in. For the job you want, is that what you need? Do you need that to have the job you're looking for?"

Definitely check in with a seasoned mentor or someone who has the job you hope to have in five years. "You need to be smart about it and ask other people in the field," adds Crawford. "Ask, 'Did you do this?' If it's something that you can put on your résumé, and if it's something that's in your field of interest, learn about it. Something as intense and expensive as, say, an MBA, you want to make sure that that's the route you want to go. Do you know the field you want to work in, and is an MBA either going to help you break into that field or move you forward in it? A writing class at lunch is one thing. It's a minimal investment. But a full-on MBA is different." Really assessing where it is that you want to be down the line will ensure that you don't waste precious time, or even more precious money, on continued education that won't get you to that vice president's chair or to the perch at the top of a national magazine.

Consider Your Options

The options for extending your education are vast: everything from company-sponsored training and local continuing education classes to full-blown master's degree programs. Research all your options. To start with, here are a few things to check out:

Tuition reimbursement. Ask your boss or human resources department about how your company invests in the futures of its employees: Is partial, or possibly full, tuition reimbursement an option? What exactly is covered? Are you required to stay with the company for a certain number of years if you take advantage of this option? Normally, tuition reimbursement applies to degree-seekers, but often companies will pay a percentage of any type of career development, as long as it's somehow related to your job or future position in the company. Basically, the company needs to see how it benefits from paying for you to go back to school. Most likely, some sort of approval from human resources or your boss is required, so figure out those details before enrolling.

Community college courses. Don't sneer at this option; you're not that high and mighty yet! The additional skills you need—a simple accounting class, an inspirational painting course, or a practical economics class—could be available very cheaply and conveniently at the local junior college. You even might be able to take a class or get certain certifications online.

Company-sponsored career development. Most large companies, especially ones that value career development for their employees, likely have some sort of program, whether it be lunchtime courses about technology or a purely creative, monthly curriculum. Ask others around your office if there's anything like this, or simply check the bulletin board in the break room for flyers.

Continuing education from local organizations. I used to take art classes in everything from stained-glass to batiking, and it really contributed to my overall creativity—inside and outside the office. Check local newspapers or newsletters for classes that might not necessarily contribute directly to your professional development but will, at the least, assuage your overall sanity and creativity.

Conferences and conventions. What appropriate organizations have educational conferences in your industry? Attending one is especially great for your leadership development, and it's likely that your company would be very happy to send you for the knowledge you'd undoubtedly bring back to share with the office.

On the Job
· · · · ·

Scenario: Your bachelor's degree was enough to get you your entry-level accounting job, but you've quickly realized you're not going much further without more knowledge of specialized areas. You realize your deficits, but how exactly do you go about fixing them?

✳

Quick Fix: Talk to your mentor, who will have helpful, unbiased advice. Did she take additional business courses after starting an entry-level position? Is that the norm? How did she keep up? What would she suggest?

Real-Life "Betty"

"As much as I complain about writing papers and doing massive amounts of reading, I can't seem to stay away from school, even with my full-time job in the international office of a private university. I didn't plan on starting a grad program right away, but this job basically allows me to earn a master's for free. I decided it was too good an opportunity to pass up! The graduate degree I am working toward isn't exactly related to my job, but I am always thinking about ways I can apply what I am learning in the classroom to my job. Plus, the degree is proving invaluable as I embark on a new endeavor: starting a nonprofit. As for the future, I'm not certain what route I will take, but I know the knowledge I am gaining makes me more well-rounded and better prepared for whatever I might encounter."

—Lauren, 25, Des Moines, Iowa

• • • • • •

To-Do List

* **Do it now**! Now is the perfect time to knock out any additional degrees that you want. If you start a family, you probably won't have much free time to take night or weekend classes.

* **Clarify your career goals**. Then see what kind of time you might have available to continue your education and reach those goals.

* **Bug your mentor or your boss**. Even if you're not sure of what exactly you'd like to do, check in with someone who's been in your position before and can advise you about a smart direction.

* **Explore all your options**. Check out options for continuing your education, including your company's tuition reimbursement, courses at local community colleges, company-sponsored programs, local trade courses, and industry conventions.

Part Five

Advance Your Career

Ask for What You Want

"It's pretty simple really. I, uh, I think I deserve a raise. I'm scheduled to get one in six months, but I'd like that to be moved up to now."

—*Darryl Philbin, a warehouse worker at Dunder Mifflin, asking boss Michael Scott for a pay bump, on* The Office

Ask and you shall receive. That axiom gets flung around quite often, but does it hold up, especially in the workplace? In the context of your career, more often than not, it does. In the case of *The Office*'s Dunder Mifflin employee Darryl, referenced above, his compensation grievances stemmed from the fact that one of his coworkers had recently been fired and he was saddled with more work than before. You might think that management would automatically recognize that he deserves a pay bump. But with the dozens of other things your boss is dealing with, it's unlikely that he will have any idea what's bugging you until you make it known.

So it comes back to the virtue of asking. In this case, we never found out whether Darryl actually got that additional 10 percent he was seeking, but the mere fact that he asked showed his initiative and immediately let his superior know what he was after. Going after what you want in the office—and making that clearly known—is important and shouldn't be limited to issues such as compensation. What about asking for a title change, an expense account, or a company car? A promotion? A transfer? These are all important things that will get swept under the rug, unless you pipe up.

Express Yourself

One of the biggest mistakes young professionals make is assuming that their bosses can read their minds. If you're suffering in silence over your lack of overtime pay or recognition, how can you expect your boss, or anyone around you at your work, to know how you're feeling? Just look at the success Betty has had with advocating for herself: After a freelance writer flaked out of an assignment, her boss Daniel Meade asked for a list of freelancers rather than tapping her for the project. Instead, Betty quickly—and in a savvy fashion—requested the chance to take a stab at the assignment. Take a note from her gumption! "Be clear about your goals and aspirations," says career coach John McKee. "It's so important."

After years of collaborating with bosses across a variety of industries, McKee has seen many valued employees leave in a huff, and their superiors didn't know they were upset in the first place. "Bosses tell me all the time, 'had she told me that she wanted that before she quit, I probably could have done something,'" McKee adds. "They say it was a total surprise—'All of a sudden he got cranky with me when he didn't get the opportunities that he wanted.'"

Have Some Rhyme to Your Reasons

The cold, hard fact of the matter is that no one else is going to go to bat for you, especially at this young stage of your career. Don't see it as being aggressive, just think about it as going after what you want and deserve. Here are a few things to think about when asking for things that'll change your career:

Select the right time. Timing is everything—and there is definitely a right and wrong time to make certain demands. Unless you're planning a birthday party, the office isn't generally the place for surprises. Sensitive requests that pertain to the advancement of your career should be discussed in a meeting. By setting up an appropriate time to chat, your boss will see you as professional and likely be more open to hearing your request.

Each instance is different, but generally wait until your boss is in a good mood or seems open for a chat. Obviously, avoid bringing up sensitive issues when a big deadline or project is looming, or when you're upset and simply reacting to a bad situation. For example, asking for a raise just after your company has announced layoffs and a bad quarter is silly. On that same note, the perfect time may be when there is a great demand for the services you provide. Can you easily get a job elsewhere? Do you have an offer in hand? In those instances, you've got to ask right away.

Go to the right person. Figure out who should hear your request. There's no point in making requests for more responsibility or an additional vacation day if they fall on deaf ears. Most likely, your direct boss is the person you should bring your issues to. Going over your boss's head is a last resort; it shows insubordination. "I prefer that my employees talk to me before going to the overall boss," says editor-in-chief Deborah Ohrn. "I try to resolve the issue first, and if I can't, I take it up through the appropriate channels."

Do your research. When asking for what you want—be it a pay raise, a promotion, or something as simple as a day off—make sure you've got all your facts straight. If it's something like a raise, have facts and figures ready to go that prove you deserve more. For something as simple as a vacation day, just make sure that it's not at the same time as a conference you're required to attend or a week when everyone else will be out of the office. When you can say, "Well, I already looked into that, and here's what I know," it shows your boss you've put thought into what you're asking for.

In my first real post-collegiate job, I was an editorial assistant at a custom-published television magazine. We had a small staff, and I was the youngest, so I was automatically hired at the lowest rung. However, even just six months into the position, I clearly was doing much more than what my title reflected, so I scheduled a time to chat with my boss to talk about fixing that. I presented what I knew—that the tasks I was carrying out every day were on the level of an associate editor at publications X, Y, and Z—and it helped me get the credit I wanted and deserved.

Lose the entitlement. Is what you want realistic? Today's fast-paced career world has lulled many young professionals into believing that they deserve everything now. That attitude generally won't fly with a baby boomer in the room, especially if they slogged away in the trenches for a lot longer than you did. Going back to Betty's situation, remember and heed her slow progression toward asking for writing assignments—she had been at *Mode* for a season and a half before she started really advocating for herself. Patience is a virtue!

"Young, driven, career-minded folks are making most people in their 40s and older crazy because they have a greater sense of entitlement, or they're seen as having a greater sense of entitlement." McKee says. "You're seen as having more demanding expectations for career movement and pay. They're called millennial concerns." The difference between asking for what you want and coming off as a prima donna is a fine line, so give yourself a reality check before making what could be a big mistake.

On the Job
· · · · ·

Scenario: Nearly a year into your job as a marketing assistant, you realize you're doing the exact same work as the marketing associate who's got a better title than you. More than anything—even more than a raise—you just want to be recognized for your contributions with the correct title, especially because it will enhance your résumé. How do you elegantly ask for a title change?

✳

Quick Fix: Ideally, you'd talk to your boss about this during an annual review, but if that's months down the line, schedule a meeting with your boss and be clear about your intentions. But before you walk in for the talk, do your research and come in with a plan. Bring a brag list that includes a list of your achievements; any additional education or responsibilities you've acquired during your time at the company; and emails or notes from clients, coworkers, or direct reports that illuminate your efforts. Go into the meeting with confidence and outline why you deserve the enhanced title, backed up by your brag list. As long as you've earned it, your boss will be hard-pressed to say no.

Real-Life "Betty"

"I was interviewing for a lower midrange position that I really wanted, but I knew I was worth more than what they were offering, which was about 10 percent less than I made at my previous job. I was honest with the HR rep and told her politely that I couldn't take the job at that salary. The next day, I got a call from my potential boss, who asked if I would take the job at the same pay as my old job. As nice as it was that they upped their offer, I really wanted more, and I told her so. Then she asked me for an exact number. I decided to ask for about 30 percent more than their original offer, thinking I might be able to get 15 to 20 percent more after we bargained. I was willing my voice not to waver. I named my number, and after an excruciating minute of silence, she said she'd get back to me, and she hung up.

"Twenty minutes later, she called and just said, 'OK. See you Monday.' I couldn't believe it! I'd gotten exactly what I'd asked for, which was much more than I expected. Who knew that doing some background research, knowing your worth, standing fast, and—most importantly—asking for exactly what I wanted could work in salary negotiations? I realized that employers are probably not going to retract an offer because you asked for more money—more likely they'll respect you for it, and tell you what's possible."

—Melissa, 30, Brooklyn, New York

• • • • • •

To-Do List

* **Confidently ask for what you want**. Don't expect your boss to know what you want out of your job. You've got to put that on the table clearly.

* **Have a plan**. When you're asking for something, have a plan: choose the right time, do your research, and have your facts straight.

* **Be cool**. If you're nervous when piping up for yourself, it'll show. As we discussed in earlier chapters, body language makes a huge difference in projecting confidence. If you don't have confidence in yourself, your boss won't either.

* **Be your own best advocate**. No one is going to do it for you!

Embrace Networking

"So I spent the entire evening just networking and giving out my business cards. Anyway, it was really fun, and I finally felt like I belonged."

—*Betty Suarez, telling her sister Hilda about an evening spent making connections at The Rack, on* Ugly Betty

Out of all the magazines she could have worked at in New York City, *Mode* was never *Ugly Betty*'s Betty Suarez's first choice. Granted, she is just lucky to have a job in such a cutthroat industry, but to her professional-advancement smarts, she's always seen her current job as a pit stop on the way to something else. So it was no surprise when she stepped out only a few weeks into her job to do some networking with other people in her field: people who could potentially help her land a job at her dream magazine someday down the road.

While her coworkers Amanda and Marc may have mocked her for handing out her business cards and getting chummy with the other assistants at The Rack that evening, Betty couldn't have been more spot-on with her tactics. Who knows what may come of the connections she made? Could be that one of those people she gave her business card to and chatted with for ten minutes remembers her in three years when they're looking for a mid-level editor. Or, could be that one of them asks her to write a freelance article for their magazine next week. Either way, Betty shrewdly embraced networking as essential to advancing her career, and you should too.

Learn the Power of Networking

"On a global basis, the research is pretty clear that people get jobs through connections," says career coach John McKee. "Like probably in the 75 percent range, in business." What he's saying is that you're more likely to get your next job through someone you know. Don't know anyone? That's a big problem.

Career coach Hallie Crawford chimes in on the subject too. "Networking is huge," she adds. "I think there's nothing like it, and it's a vital part of the job search." Career experts can't extol enough on the virtues of how building professional connections helps with job searching. "Networking is critical," says career expert Dan King. "Most employers have an internal job posting system, but it's a bullshit process. They've already decided who's going to take the job. Often, they're posting jobs to solicit résumés so they can say they've done an exhaustive search from a wide demographic."

Most importantly, though, remember that networking isn't something to do here and there; it's a careerlong process of building relationships and getting to know people who may be able to help you down the road. And, hopefully, you can help them out one day too. You might make a friend or two, as well. "When I say network, your best time to network is not when you're looking for a job," says King. "You should make a point where you say you want to meet one new person a week at your current job. Join task forces and committees, because the more people who know you and you have within your network of acquaintances, the easier it is to express your interest when an opportunity arises. Even if they're not the hiring manager, they can probably put in a good word for you because they know who you are."

Never "Work" a Room

Note: Networking is not being smarmy, taking a business card, and making small talk. "We have this distaste for going out and working a room, and if we think that's what networking is, we're wrong," King says. "The stronger your network, the better."

"People who are not mixers say, 'I can't imagine going out and schmoozing,' but my advice is to just give yourself a goal. If you're the shy, quiet type, go out there and say, 'I just want to have conversations with two people and if I've done that, good,' says King. Forget the other people who are working the room. If you have good, solid conversations with two people, you've done well. If you go into those situations feeling shy and comfortable, look for someone who's looking the same way. Go over and introduce yourself to that person. They'll be happy and you won't be standing alone. When someone is feeling shy and uncomfortable, and you come over and introduce yourself, they don't forget you."

Seek Connections

Think about all the people you come into contact with on a daily basis at work. Do you really know all of them? How many people do you exclusively communicate with via email that you've never met? Realize those in your orbit you should know, and seek out other new professional contacts using the following resources:

Tap people you already know. This worked for *Friends'* Rachel Green when she got a job at Ralph Lauren through her friend Mark. The wisdom is to use the connections you already have at your disposal: "Tap anyone you know— friends, family," Crawford says. "Even if they don't know someone or they're not in your field, they might know someone else or they might refer you to someone else."

Solicit people at your company. "You want to have visibility with people in related areas who could invite you to join them and move up the organization more quickly," McKee says. As for other ways to connect with people in other departments of your company, "Go out for coffee, go out for drinks, have lunches, get to know as many people in your peer group around the company," suggests editor-in-chief Deborah Ohrn. "Because, should you not make the 'Save List' during layoffs, what are the other opportunities where you could be saved in another group? I've seen that happen a lot too, where you've got a reorganization and suddenly three or four people are saved and they go to different groups." Robin on *How I Met Your Mother* was promoted from reporter to on-air anchor for playing nice, and making friends with one of her coworkers, who suggested her specifically for the position.

Go online. "Obviously, MySpace, Facebook, and LinkedIn are great tools to use," McKee says. "LinkedIn is probably one of the first choices of recruiters and people who are looking for other folks." Instead of just posting a profile and doing nothing more with it, see about finding people who have jobs you'd like and send them a note or add them to your network. But remember, these sites are not a replacement for actual relationships; instead, view them as the catalyst for starting relationships."

Join a professional group. For me, this has been the best way to meet friends and helpful professional contacts. Since I graduated, I've worked with a networking group called Ed2010 that helps young editors find their dream jobs. We sponsor happy hours for industry types, distribute underground job postings, and put on educational panels. I got one of my post-collegiate jobs directly through one of the people I work with in the organization. More than anything, though, I've collected a great group of friends, and maybe, just maybe, they'll come in handy down the road professionally.

On the Job
· · · · ·

Scenario: You love your work, but you're dying to get this position at a company across town. You've tried applying through human resources, but it's a black hole of failed attempts. How do you get some traction at the company?

✳

Quick Fix: Think about who you know who works in that company, even if they don't work in the department you're applying to. Give your contact a ring to see if she knows someone who'd take your résumé directly. Does she have any advice? Maybe your friend can even put in a good word, and if so, the job is likely yours.

Real-Life "Betty"

"From nearly the first day of business school, I was inundated with all kinds of networking events. For the most part, I thought they were silly. Recruiters would show up and wow all of us students, and I'd politely take their cards. But a funny thing happened: I met a few of these recruiters that I actually got along with well. So I shot a few of them an email the day after meeting, and I'd keep them apprised of my progress through school every now and then. I guess now that I look back, I knew what I was doing, because come graduation two years later, the contacts I had made turned into glistening job offers. The best part was that I didn't have to just take any job that I could find. With all the networking I had done, I was lucky enough to have the pick of the litter, so to speak, when it came to my first post-business-school job."

—*James, 28, New York City*

• • • • • •

To-Do List

* **Shake off your ideas about what networking is**. It's not about being smarmy and "working" a room; it's about building lasting professional relationships.

* **Make contacts**. The ways are endless—through people you know, coworkers in other departments at work, online, at professional gatherings.

* **Follow up**. When you do meet someone you think could be a potential professional contact, grab his card and follow up. Don't think just because you have his contact info that you can come calling in five years for a job. Keep in contact from the moment you meet.

* **Give yourself a goal**. When you're at an event where people are obviously networking, give yourself an attainable goal. Tell yourself you've got to meet two people that evening, or, if you're feeling ambitious, five people!

* **Join a professional group**. Seriously, this is the best way to meet other professionals who'll help you find your next job or purchase the services you're selling. Or, they'll just become good friends, which is nice too.

Explore Every Opportunity

"A painting fellowship? In California?"

—Marshall Eriksen, reacting to his girlfriend Lily Aldrin's
desire to quit her job teaching kindergarten to explore an
artsy passion, on How I Met Your Mother

Five-year plans are great. They give you direction, goals, and, most importantly, a road map of how your future will hopefully unfold in front of you. The downside? They can lead to a blinders mentality, where you're unwilling to take a leap of faith now and then that could be the veritable feather in your career hat. Kindergarten teacher Lily Aldrin on *How I Met Your Mother* is a good example of a young professional who shook up her career a bit by pursuing a passion. Always interested in art, Lily applied for, and was granted, a painting fellowship in San Francisco. The thing was, she lived in New York City. The repercussions on her relationship with boyfriend Marshall aside—and the fact that she quickly came back after realizing she belonged in Manhattan—this exploration of a new avenue in her career is one to be imitated in even your career. It's always good to explore something new, within reason, if it could take you farther professionally.

To take it even further and ground it in reality, exploring new opportunities shouldn't be limited to the ones you have outlined in your too-rigid five- or ten-year plan. Sometimes, the best options are the ones you didn't plan for, like making the switch from one area of your company to another or even moving into a different, but possibly related, field than where you're currently working. Whatever your path is, make sure to never snub an option; you never know to what great possibilities it could lead.

Times Have Changed

For better or for worse, today's working world is much different than the one our parents, and most of our college professors and bosses, grew up in. Corporate structures are different, multitasking has led to widely diverse positions, bouncing from one job to the next is considered the norm, and telecommuting is all the rage.

More than anything, though, this means the opportunities for you to manage your career however you like are endless. And, most importantly: There is no right or wrong path! That freedom to test out new possibilities when it comes to your career is what will likely help you get farther than your boss in much less time than she did. Dr. Randall Hansen, founder of QuintessentialCareers.com and marketing professor at

Stetson University in DeLand, Florida, explains: "A generation ago, all corporations had these career ladders. It was really a step-by-step process across the board in organizations."

Unfortunately for the drones who were employed, that led to a cookie-cutter career. "You'd go from worker to assistant manager to manager to group manager to area manager," Dr. Hansen adds. "You had these ladders you followed, so theirs was a very direct career path."

Fortunately, "In the last decade or so with all the downsizing and right-sizing and mergers and whatnot, all these ladders have been crushed. A lot of times there is not a direct path, so you do have to take some other kind of route that's not quite the straight path that you were going down."

Keep Your Eyes and Ears Open

"If someone approaches you and says, 'We think this would be good for you,' you should definitely explore it, if for nothing else than for the value of respecting that contact," says Dr. Hansen. That tactic certainly worked for Betty, who jumped ship at *Mode* to go to another magazine at Meade Publications. She was back at *Mode* before long, but she was willing to entertain the notion of trying something new. In the end, she's better from the experience. As they say, what doesn't kill you only makes you stronger. "If it doesn't work out, they might come back down the line and have something that's perfect for you. You have to explore, especially in changing industries like technology or media, because you don't know if your job or the job you aspire to have will exist in five years. A lot of these standard promotions up a ladder also don't exist because organizations are flattening. So you may have to step aside until you can come back in the position you want. Check out what comes your way and avoid being stuck to such a rigid plan."

While doling out this advice, Dr. Hansen cautions to avoid being reckless with your decisions. "Be careful, because I've definitely talked to a lot of workers who made mistakes," he warns. "They may have made a lateral move or moves they thought were better for them, or maybe they were forced into a move because of downsizing, where they were told you can either leave or switch to this area. Now, they are totally lost in an area that they're not passionate about and don't know how to get back to where they started."

Shop Around

Studies show that today's young professionals will likely have several career changes in their lifetime—not just job switches, but full-blown new careers. But, luckily for you, when you're young you have more flexibility with pursuing new opportunities than later, when you have things such as a mortgage payment, a spouse, and possibly a child.

Career coach Maria Marsala even took a serpentine route to get where she is today. She worked on Wall Street early in her career. "I was very open to whatever came my way because I had no direction, so I tried a lot of different things: from working in my own neighborhood to selling Avon," she says. "But I always looked for an opportunity to learn something new and who would have thought I would have been passionate about fixed-income securities? It wasn't on my list." Had Maria never given finance a chance, she would not have discovered a job that she was stellar at and very much enjoyed.

On the Job
· · · · ·

Scenario: Ever since you were a child, you knew you'd probably join your dad's business in some capacity after college. Now, two years after graduation, you're on his sales team, cutting deals for his dog food company. But a good friend who does marketing says he can get you a sweet job on his team of a large corporation. You'd get to travel, work with a variety of clients, and maybe even have a few lackeys report to you. Do you immediately turn down the offer, or see what's up?

✳

Quick Fix: If you've learned anything from this chapter, the wisdom is to explore the possibility that you've been presented with. What kind of clients would you work with? What are the perks? Would you be promoted quickly? How does your dad feel about it? Would you get better experience than at your dad's small company? Another thought is that you could go work for the big dogs for a while, then bring all your high-falutin' knowledge back to the company in a few years and take it to the next level. Ultimately, you have to decide if it's the right fit, but don't immediately dismiss the idea—it could be the stepping-stone to your perfect job down the road.

Real-Life "Betty"

"Since graduation, I have explored and applied liberally for awesome jobs. This approach has found me writing countless cover letters and reformatting my résumé—but it has paid off. The flexibility of being right out of college, the willingness to take on new adventures, and having supportive friends and family has enabled me to pack up and go in two weeks' (or less) notice for the right opportunity. In the three years after graduation, I had four different jobs that required a quick move and relocation. I'll be honest, one of the four opportunities was a bust, but I still don't regret taking the chance. The others found me sailing across the Indian Ocean, hanging out with presidential candidates in Iowa, and traveling across America."

—*Mark, 25, Des Moines, Iowa*

• • • • • •

To-Do List

* **Break out**! Never think that you have to follow one specific career track or stick to something that you outlined when you were in college. Some of your best opportunities might be the ones that seem odd at first.

* **Embrace change**. Joining a committee you thought you wouldn't be interested in? Taking on that extra

task outside of your expertise? It may lead you to discover a new direction for your career.

* **Keep your options open**. You never know what might be coming your way.

LESSON 24

Snag a Promotion

"This is your chance. Go after that job, Mary! Take the pieces of your life and put them together."

—*Phyllis Lindstrom, encouraging Mary to go after Lou Grant's old job, on* The Mary Tyler Moore Show

When it comes to your career, few things are more fulfilling than the moment you're told you're being promoted. Hello pay raise and a better title! So let's talk about how you can make that happen. Truly, in one way or another, most of this book is focused on advice that'll help you leap to that next step beyond your entry-level position. But, specifically, there's always more you can do.

As the above quote illustrates, when Mary was up for Mr. Grant's job on *The Mary Tyler Moore Show*, her girlfriends Phyllis and Rhoda insisted that she put herself in the running. At first, Mary was convinced she didn't want the job. Later, she realized she was already doing everything the job entailed, which is just what she should have been doing as a productive employee. "Listen, you two don't understand," she exclaimed. "This job is going to mean coming in early, staying late, working straight through lunch hours, taking care of a million details, keeping the sponsors happy, working late. It's… exactly what I do now."

For starters, you can try those same principles that made Mary such a valuable asset around the WJM-TV newsroom. Ultimately, she didn't end up getting the job because Mr. Grant took back his old position, but she was more than qualified and did what any young professional in her situation should—she went after the position.

Go for It!

Sounds easy, right? Well, not so fast. Keep in mind that you shouldn't just suddenly snap into I-want-a-promotion mode. Getting promoted is something you should be working on from day one. I've explained some of these ideas before, but let's go over them again. With the help of career expert Dr. Randall Hansen, here are five surefire ways to leap up the ladder at your workplace:

Volunteer for additional assignments. Bosses love their employees who pitch in without question. Think of *Ugly Betty's* go-getter Betty Suarez: She never turned down any assignment—whether it was putting on a ridiculous outfit at a photo shoot or coming up with a new cover concept for *Mode*. "If you're in a meeting and someone throws out some idea that's beyond your current purview or might require some work after hours, volunteer for that," says Dr. Hansen. "If you do, it shows initiative, especially if it's the boss's pet project. If you do well, it's immediately going to raise your standing in the organization."

Jumping in where you don't have expertise may be scary, but spend the time studying up, and avoid being one of those whiny people who always turn down offers that'll make you shine. "I've found a lot of younger job seekers see that as more of a burden than an opportunity," Dr. Hansen continues. "It's an opportunity for you to say, 'Hey, I'm here, and I'll do what it takes. At a moment's notice, I'll fly to the Chicago office and fill in for this meeting.' I knew a student who graduated a year ago and went to a company in Pennsylvania, and on his third day, they asked him if he had a passport. They flew him out to their London office for a week. He jumped on it, and now a year later he's been quite successful and has been promoted with a nice salary bump. It's *the* way to get noticed, especially early on when you're making that first impression."

Be a team player. "Not all companies work in teams, but in situations where you are on a temporary or permanent team, be a good team player," Dr. Hansen suggests. "Do the work, but walk that fine line between wanting people to know what you did but also touting that it was a team effort. You'll be seen as a person who's more valuable because you're not just the big ego, but you're also showing that it wouldn't be done without the team's effort."

Find a mentor at your company. A mentor inside or outside your company is great, but if you're trying to get promoted in your current position, consider finding a mentor inside your company who preferably had your position in the past. Do like Ellen Parsons did on *Damages* with seasoned lawyer Tom Shayes. She sought him out as a resource, and she eventually acquired more responsibility and even an assistant of her own. Additionally, Dr. Hansen says, "They can whisper in other people's ears and say, 'You know, this person is ready for the next step.'" Whether good or not, Shayes certainly had the ear of Ellen's boss.

How do you get a mentor? "The best way for that is typically through more informal stuff," Dr. Hansen continues. "It might be at a company retreat or it might be through the social or sporting events that organizations oftentimes put together. You can meet someone and if it clicks, then you can ask that person if he or she would be a mentor to you and help you in your career. It's a nice recognition of the person too."

Have face time with your boss. During much of your day-to-day duties, you'll find yourself working mostly with coworkers or even other superiors who might not have much to do directly with you getting promoted. If that's the case, schedule regular sit-down meetings with your direct boss. Betty talks to her boss frequently, and *30 Rock*'s Liz Lemon is always in Jack Donaghy's office talking about the future, among other things. "Chat about where you are in your career and what you've accomplished," Dr. Hansen says. "Obviously, you'll do that at an annual review, but it's a good thing to do, especially if you perform work that's not totally in front of your boss. You should let them know what you're doing and check in on a regular basis so he or she is aware of your accomplishments. You don't want to walk in and be like, 'Hey, I want to be promoted tomorrow.'"

Self-promote. Try your best not to be totally shameless about it, but make sure that everyone, especially your boss, is totally aware of your accomplishments and contributions. "Do a little self-marketing or self-promotion, but not in a very overt way, so that your boss knows what you're doing," Dr. Hansen advises. "If you're doing something that's a little outside of the eye of the boss—say if you're working on a team that's cross-departmental—it could be something where you go to the boss's office or it may be something that's informal where you go out to lunch or chat at a social event. You also could drop your boss an update email to let him or her know where you stand on projects, like a status report. If you feel like you're underutilized, make it clear that you think you have the capacity to do a few more things. It shows initiative and is self-promotion without being too pushy."

On the Job
• • • • •

Scenario: You're working on a cross-departmental project that your boss knows you're doing but is not directly involved with. You think your performance is good, so good, in fact, it could lead to a promotion for you soon. How do you let your boss know?

✱

Quick Fix: Here's a little trick: Use email. It sounds a tad scary, but send a status report about the project to the others working on the project and copy your boss. Applaud the team's work. In doing so, you're also applauding yourself, and your boss will definitely take note. The beauty is that it's shrewdly veiled as a "Just keeping you updated!" note.

Real-Life "Betty"

"Only a few months after college, I scored my dream job working as an editorial assistant at a midsize magazine in New York City. Fortunately, I was able to do a little bit of everything in this entry-level position. Shortly after I started, the magazine's website was relaunched and help was needed. Eager to chip in, I was trained on the technology and quickly given a few duties of my own. Over the next year, more money was allocated to the site, which meant it needed more staff. Eager to get promoted out of my assistant position, I stayed persistent. I attended meetings about the website and kept my current boss apprised of all my additional duties. I befriended the website director for her guidance. I wanted to be promoted onto the website—and not in the position of an assistant! I realized that position was a good opportunity for me. Because of my tenacity and willingness to jump right in, I was offered the position and even leaped past some of my coworkers in terms of responsibilities."

—*Nathan, 25, New York City*

• • • • • •

To-Do List

* **Do more**. Even if you're already loaded up with lots to do, and especially if you're lacking tasks to handle, volunteer to take on more. Bosses rarely let those who contribute with all their might go without a promotion.

* **Contribute to the whole**. Sure, you're looking out for your own interests, but contributing wholeheartedly to the teams you're a part of shows your boss you're a team player.

* **Get advice**. You've read it in the book before: Get a mentor! Find someone who can give you advice

about your career path and tips about how to make your move up the ladder at your company.

* **Corner your boss**. Okay, don't corner your boss per se, but make sure you're clocking face time. It's valuable for your boss to know what you're doing, how you're contributing, and that you're eager for more.

* **Toot your own horn**! Make sure what you're doing is noticed. If possible, use non-smarmy tactics that smartly showcase your contributions instead of dirty tactics that make others look bad.

LESSON 25
Exit Gracefully

"I told her I was sick of her bullshit. When Patty was my age, do you think she would have tolerated a boss like her? Then why should I?"

—*Ellen Parsons, telling her mentor Hollis Nye about the fiery end to her job at Hewes & Associates, on* Damages

As much as you may love your job, your company, or your boss—or the other way around—it's inevitable that you'll have to leave at some point. Maybe it's a promotion or two down the road or maybe it's for a better gig with a new employer, but staying with one company for decades rarely happens these days. Even if you're just moving to a new department—or in Ellen's case above, totally leaving your company for good—you've simply got to have an exit strategy.

The way Ellen left Hewes & Associates, though, by telling her tyrannical boss Patty Hewes that she was full of bullshit is unadvisable, no matter what the circumstances. Besides being bad form, you never know where you may run into your old boss or coworkers again. For an example of a good resignation, look to Betty Suarez. When she left *Mode* for *MYW* magazine—

even though she was back in a matter of weeks—she gave appropriate notice, left her tasks in order, found and trained her replacement, and kept in touch with her old coworkers. When confronted with a similar situation—and you surely will be—follow in Betty's poised footsteps.

Keep It Under Wraps

Unless you're planning to use a job offer to bargain for more money or a promotion, keep the details of your job search covert until you've sealed the deal. If you have to, communicate with potential new employers via email or take a quick break to chat with them on a cell phone outside of the office. Be as discreet as possible, and try to avoid what happened to Rachel Green on *Friends*. Remember when her boss from Ralph Lauren caught her on a lunch interview with a recruiter for Gucci? Bosses don't like to know about your job searching, so in Rachel's case, she was quickly fired. Her situation was hard to avoid—Rachel had no idea she'd run into her current boss—but it serves as a lesson in keeping your job searching clandestine until you've secured a new offer.

Another sign that will tip your boss and coworkers off to your desire for a new job will be if you suddenly start dressing up for all those interviews and steal an hour or two away frequently for mysterious doctors' appointments. Just realize that those tactics are obvious, and plan ahead. If you know you'll be job searching soon, step up your wardrobe in advance, so it doesn't look like anything out of the ordinary. Plan interviews at the beginning or end of the day or over your lunch hour, so your absence is not so obvious.

Resign with Dignity

It's normal to use email, IMs, and texts for nearly any kind of communication these days, but never use those as a means to resign to your boss. First and foremost, it's tacky and unprofessional. Would you send an email to your sister about the death of one of your parents? Alright, that's a tad extreme, but quitting a job as a professional is a situation that screams for a face-to-face meeting.

When I gave notice at my first post-collegiate job, it was one of the hardest things I've ever done in my career. Actually—and I'll admit it was a mistake—I had to do it over the phone. When I got my new position at *Entertainment Weekly*, I actually was not at my current workplace but instead working on a freelance project elsewhere in New York City. Because I needed to give two weeks' notice right away, I emailed my boss asking if I could set up a time to chat that day over my lunch break. I think he immediately sensed what might be happening—it was rather clear that I was looking for a promotion or a new job—and told me to give him a call immediately. I explained that I wanted to talk in person, but my boss, being the in-person-phobe that he was, insisted on a phone call. With lots of trepidation, I called and gave him the scoop on my new position. He was understandably upset, and made me feel awful for "abandoning" him, but I was more shaken that I had to tell him over the phone. It just felt so impersonal. Still, I've learned my lesson and will *never* do that again.

The meeting you set up with your boss should be like any other that you request to update her on the status of a project. Before you go into the meeting, think about how you're going to break the news. Also, is this a case where you *want* your boss to convince you to stay? If you're leaving no matter what, tell yourself that before you go in. You'll also want to prepare a brief written statement outlining your resignation. Keep it short and sweet: You're resigning, when you're leaving, and—if you choose to include—why you're leaving. Plus, a few kind words and well wishes for the future couldn't hurt. Bosses always want a written resignation. It's a good idea to include your new work or existing personal contact information on this document, as well.

After You Resign

Following Betty's model when she left for *MYW*, here are pointers for your last two weeks:

Be happy. You've got a new job, so what's the worst that could happen in two more weeks at your current employer? "You have to leave with a smile," says career expert Dr. Randall Hansen.

Leave things in order. Trashing files or sabotaging your former employer in any way is unacceptable. Make sure all your projects are left at a stage someone else could easily pick up. Leave directions or notes, if possible.

Train the replacement. This is a courtesy. Betty found and trained former *Mode* receptionist Amanda and, if it's possible, you should do the same. You'll be remembered with an extra-special glow for not leaving your boss in the lurch.

Don't burn bridges. "You just never know where that boss that you told off today will be down the road," says Dr. Hansen. "He could all of a sudden be the VP of your new company. Then you'll really be in for it! It could even be two years down the line, but you won't be getting promoted at that company."

Send a goodbye note. On your last day, email your co-workers and bosses a message thanking them for the opportunity to work with them. Include your contact information and let them know you'd like to stay in touch.

On the Job
· · · · ·

Scenario: After spending a year displeased with your job, you score a new, higher-level position at a competing company. Your first instinct is to flip your boss the bird, quit your job on the spot, and never look back. Is this the most appropriate route to take?

✳

Quick Fix: Obviously not. Have some manners! Regardless that you might not have loved the people, they still deserve your respect. Plus, remember that you'll likely work with some of your now-former coworkers down the line. Who knows, one of them could be your boss one day! And they won't soon forget how you treated everyone when you left. So, do the right thing. Suck it up, give two weeks' notice, leave your tasks ready for someone else to take over, possibly train your replacement, and—even though you might not *love* them—keep in touch with your boss and coworkers.

Real-Life "Betty"

"It's never easy leaving your very first job out of school. Like a first boyfriend, I hold a torch for it and for all the things I learned by being there. But when I got an offer for a better position at another website, I knew it was time to say goodbye to entry-level. The day after I accepted the offer, I met with my boss to tell her the news. That was the hardest conversation I've ever had. She was surprised and probably upset that, at an understaffed company, she was about to have a lot more on her plate. I gave my two weeks' notice and spent those ten days working harder than ever. I wanted to finish all my outstanding projects, or at least get to a point where someone else could take over the tasks I'd spent the past year finessing. It was hard letting go of some things, but it felt great to write up instructions for the things I couldn't wait to be rid of! I took a LOT more lunches those last couple weeks. I exchanged goodbyes with all my coworkers and office buddies. The best part is that, because my industry feels so small, a year later, I still see them all the time. I actually work with two of my old coworkers at my current job!"

—Kate, 24, New York City

• • • • • •

To-Do List

* **Search covertly**. Don't let on to your boss that you're looking for a new job, unless you want to try to use that as leverage for a promotion or raise.

* **Tell your boss the news in person**. It's the courteous thing to do. Wouldn't you expect the same from someone who was quitting your team?

* **Put it in writing**. When you go tell your boss about your intention to leave, bring the news in writing as well and include information about your last day, reason, and ways to contact you in the future.

* **Give two weeks' notice**. Any less is unprofessional. If you really want to go above and beyond, agree to stay on until they've found a replacement. But you have to balance that with when your new employer needs you to start.

* **Stay positive**. The hard part is over once you've got the new job and given your notice. Even if you hated your current employer, you only have to stick it out for two more weeks.

* **Keep in touch**. You've probably made some friends, and—heck!—maybe you like your boss. Pass along your contact information and don't burn any bridges. You may just be working with these people again in the future.

Acknowledgments

Many thanks to my first-rate, totally patient editor Shannon Berning, without whom this book wouldn't be happening, and the rest of the team at Kaplan: Dominique Polfliet, Elizabeth Pollock, Jennifer Farthing, Jennifer Grace, Julie Marshall, Kevin Cooper, Michelle Patterson, Susan Barry, and Yvette Romero— you made this timid writer feel so welcome from day one.

A great deal of appreciation is due to all of my fine coworkers at *Entertainment Weekly* for their constant guidance through the treacherous waters of entertainment, unknowingly providing an anecdote or two, and, as always, their warm support. Specific thanks go to Henry Goldblatt for blessing this project and his constant mentorship.

A round of applause goes to all the real-life "Bettys" out there—friends, friends-of-friends, friends-of-friends-of-friends, and so on—who graciously shared stories and details of their professional lives. You are the guts of this book! To the load of experts and bosses too—thank you for your time and minds. You added much-needed gravitas to my ideas.

Find Your Inner Ugly Betty wouldn't have been possible without my personal team of enthusiasts and friends, including but certainly not limited to: Alina Dizik, Amanda Wolfe, Amy Roberts, Angela Renkoski, Archana Ram, Chandni Jhunjhunwala, Chandra Czape Turner, Colin Kearns, Emily Hendricks, Hannah Tucker, Jenn Andrlik, Jennifer Armstrong, Jessica Anderson, Katie Schmitz, Kelsey Rahn, Laura Hahn, Lexi Walters, Lindsay Soll, Lisa Freedman, Liz Owens, Mark Federoff, Meredith Bodgas, Nathan Geddie, Patricia Prijatel, Särah Goldschadt, Sara Rietsch, Shannon Tharp, Vanessa Juarez, and Youyoung Lee. You all contributed handily—whether it be indulging my late-night gripes or offering an essential suggestion—and you make me smile everyday.

Lastly, to my siblings, Tyler, Tiffany, and Tucker: Thank you for encouraging me each step of the way, and your laughter. And to Mom and Dad: I'll admit, you don't wrinkle my life anymore. I love you for your unbridled enthusiasm about this project and showing me the way all these years.

About the Author

Tanner Stransky works at *Entertainment Weekly*, where he writes stories and reviews about television, books, and movies, including frequent postings to the publication's website, EW.com. He previously clocked time at the *New York Post*, *Teen People*, and several custom-published magazines.

In addition to his full-time gig, Tanner is on staff with Ed2010, a career-focused networking group dedicated to helping young editors find their dream job in the magazine industry and continue their trek up the masthead. He also writes an entertainment column for *Figure*, a plus-size women's fashion magazine.

Hailing from Kansas, Tanner now lives in New York City.